THE FOOD DEMON INTERVIEWS

Keep Your Food Demon Out of The Driver's Seat – Defend Yourself Against Its Sneakiest Tactics

Glenn Livingston PhD

CONTENTS

INTRODUCTION

This book may change the way you think about food forever... I know that's a big promise, but I don't make it lightly! I published this book as a companion to the bestselling Never Binge Again™, a copy of which you can download for FREE in Kindle, Nook, or PDF format here: (https://neverbingeagain.com/index.php/main/readerbonuses)

Never Binge Again was originally a journal I kept about the very strange method I developed to put an end to 30 years of my own binge eating. There's a lot more to it than this, but essentially, it was me against my Inner Pig™ (my Reptilian brain)...and all the crazy things it told me to get me to repeatedly break my best laid dietary plans...

Despite numerous doctors telling me I was going to die before I was 40 years old...

Despite working with some of the best psychologists in the world (*I grew up in a family of them in and around New York City*)...

Despite having been the CEO of two consulting companies which sold more than $30,000,000 to Fortune 500 firms including many in the Big Food industry...

And despite doing my own food addiction study with more

than 40,000 people.

That's right, after 30 years of suffering, this sophisticated, ultra-experienced psychologist and jet-set businessman finally got his act together with food and maintained an approximately 60 pound weight loss...

Not by loving himself thin and/or nurturing his inner wounded child...

But by aggressively separating his constructive vs. destructive thoughts about food.

I decided whatever was off my diet was "Pig Slop™", whatever the Pig suggested as a reason I should eat it was "Pig Squeal™"... and I simply wouldn't let the Pig tell me what to do.

This method, as crude and primitive as it was, was the ONLY thing which gave me those extra microseconds at the moment of impulse to wake up, remember who I was and what my higher goals were... and make the right decision.

In any case, you should really read the original book to get the most out of this one... it has more than 1,250 reviews on Amazon and, as of this publication, more than 80% were four stars or better!

What THIS book contains is a series of word for word transcripts from actual coaching interviews... along with links to the blog post where you can HEAR the recording. It's a great way to get a sense of how this all works in practice after you understand it in principle.

That said, without further ado, here are the Food Demon Interviews!

CHAPTER 1: GETTING BACK ON TRACK AFTER A PERIOD OF BINGING

Introduction

Denise is a successful client who fell off track for a little while and gained a little weight back. Her Pig™ kept telling her she could "start again tomorrow" AND "it's so unfair you have to be different than the rest of your family" AND "it's going to take SO long to reach your goal there's no reason to even bother" AND "just one bite won't hurt" …but as most of you know by now, these are ALL nonsensical Pig Squeals™! Listen to the interview to see how easily we put Denise's Pig back in its cage with a short, focused coaching session!

Interview Audio

https://www.neverbingeagain.com/TheBlog/recorded-sessions/getting-back-on-track-after-a-period-of-binging/

Things to watch for in this interview:

- How to deal with the "I'll start tomorrow" Pig squeal
- How to deal with the "My family is eating this and I should be able to as well" Pig squeal
- How to deal with the "It's going to take me so long to get to my goal weight – so why bother" squeal
- How to create a motivating vision of the future that will compel you to cage your Pig
- How to deal with the "One bite won't hurt" squeal

Interview Begins Here

Dr. Glenn: Tell me how things have been going.

Denise: Things were going really well at first. I had lost almost 20 pounds, and then I went back to the same old regimen of "I'll start tomorrow, I'll start tomorrow, I'll start tomorrow." I've taken it back to step one again, and I'm re-reading the book and trying to get back to caging my inner Pig.

Dr. Glenn: You had a reversal of intent and then you decided that you would just wait to start tomorrow. That's a difficulty that a lot of people have. Is there any change to your food plan? Do you need to review it, or are you perfectly comfortable that you really know what healthy eating is?

Denise: I really know what healthy eating looks like, and I know what I can and can't do. Part of the problem for me is that my kids and husband are only eating some of what I'm eating because obviously they don't have the same issues with food as I do. That trips me up sometimes.

Dr. Glenn: Your family is eating what would be Pig slop to you?

Denise: Exactly.

Dr. Glenn: There are a couple of Pig squeals that we're getting here. One is the "I'll start tomorrow" squeal and the other is that the family is eating Pig slop, in your definition of the word. So, what's the rest of that squeal? Your family is eating Pig slop and therefore...?

Denise: I should be able to eat it too. Why do I have to be different? The other squeal is it's going to take me so long to get to where I want to be, so why bother?

Dr. Glenn: What else has your Pig been saying to keep you binging?

Denise: That you can have just one bite. It all comes back to "I can start tomorrow," and then I just pretty much let go of everything. "Why bother?" is the other one.

Dr. Glenn: Let's go back and revisit "Why bother?" I know you've done this before, but if you were to eat perfectly healthy according to your food plan for a year, can you tell me what would be different in your life?

Denise: I would feel better in my own skin. I would just have a healthier outlook. I wouldn't hide behind my weight. I would just really enjoy life because I think I use my weight as a barrier.

Dr. Glenn: If I were to observe you all day long a year from now as opposed to right now when you're hiding behind your weight, what would I see?

Denise: This is going to sound like a pun, but I would be lighter. Not just the weight, but my soul would be lighter.

Dr. Glenn: What would you be able to do?

Denise: Anything that I would want to do. I wouldn't have to worry about whether something will fit me. I wouldn't have to worry about what my next meal would be or how to get my next fix. I'd be able to be me.

Dr. Glenn: Who is "you"? I know that sounds like a silly question, but one of the ways that our Pigs make Pig slop seem more appealing is by preventing us from seeing who we are and who we really want to be. Maybe there was a time in your life when you were eating healthy and you felt more like yourself. Could you tell me about that?

Denise: When I'm getting down to who I really am, I just feel free. I feel as if I don't have any barriers around me. Whatever that may be or whoever I may be, it's as if the walls have come down and I am okay with who I am. I don't have to try to be something that I'm not.

Dr. Glenn: And when you're eating Pig slop, what do you feel like you have to try to be?

Denise: Perfect. I give up at that point. I'm a person who gives up.

Dr. Glenn: You just really don't feel accepted when you're heavier and you just can't be yourself. You feel judged. And when you're thin and eating healthy, you can be more present with other people. Does that mean you look them in the eye more? That you're more available to hug them or smile or laugh?

Denise: It sounds corny, but I'm just more available to be me. I don't have any barriers up to who I am.

Dr. Glenn: Is that what you mean by "I'd feel better in my own skin"?

Denise: Yes. I wouldn't have to be hiding behind the walls. I think I hide behind the Pig.

Dr. Glenn: What about your health? Is there anything physically that would improve?

Denise: My blood pressure. I'd get back into shape.

Dr. Glenn: Why is it important to you to improve your blood pressure?

Denise: I can possibly live longer. I know it sounds contrite right now, but that's really what it comes down to.

Dr. Glenn: It sounds contrite to our Pigs, but it's important to us. Why do you want to live longer? What would you do with that time?

Denise: Just be free. I know I keep saying this, but I'd not be living behind this wall and trying to get my next fix. I would be able to not have that be the focus of everything I do.

Dr. Glenn:　A lot of people say that the Pig has cheated them out of a lot of years of life.

Denise:　Absolutely, without a doubt.

Dr. Glenn:　Maybe you can't get those years back, but you could live the balance of your life being free and being yourself.

Denise:　It wouldn't be the center of everything I do and everything I say and everywhere I go.

Dr. Glenn:　How important is that to you?

Denise:　Really, it's the most important thing.

Dr. Glenn:　The most important driver for you is to be able to be yourself again.

Denise:　Yes, and not having the eating be the first and foremost thing in my life.

Dr. Glenn:　Are there clothes that you would wear or meetings that you would take that you're not taking now?

Denise:　There are definitely clothes that I would wear. I don't really have anything specific. I just want to feel comfortable. As for meetings that I would take, I'd break out of my shell more with the jewelry that I make and try to go out and showcase it. The stuff that I make is really nice and a lot of the time I don't get out there and try to find a venue to sell it because of this barrier.

Denise:　I used to love to get dressed up and have on necklaces and other jewelry. I don't do that anymore. When I was in a place where the Pig was caged, I was doing that again. Even though I had weight that I had to lose, I felt like I was at peace again.

Dr. Glenn:　You'd break more out of your shell. You'd be more at peace. Being more at peace is much more important than all of these other things you're talking about.

Denise: Yes, being more at peace and being able to be myself. I just want to be at peace.

Dr. Glenn: Since you have a visual image of being at peace with those necklaces, could you describe one for me? Maybe there's a particular necklace that you wore that you were starting to feel more at peace with and you were smiling and happy with yourself as you started to wear it.

Denise: Actually, I have two that I really like. There's a deep hot pink and silver necklace that I would wear a lot, and another jade-looking one that I would wear too.

Dr. Glenn: What do you wear the hot pink and silver necklace with? Is there a nice dress that you like?

Denise: I could wear it either with jeans or dressing up.

Dr. Glenn: It sounds cool. What about the jade one?

Denise: Same thing.

Dr. Glenn: Does the ability to get out of your shell more have any financial impact on you?

Denise: Yes. It would have a financial impact because I would be able to start to contribute more to the family and also not be spending the money on food.

Dr. Glenn: If you had to conservatively quantify that, how much would it be worth for you?

Denise: Just on the eating alone, I would say probably $100 a week going through drive-throughs.

Dr. Glenn: That's about $5,200 a year that you'd save.

Denise: That'd be a nice little vacation for everybody.

Dr. Glenn: And would you make any extra money because you were getting out there with your jewelry?

Denise: Absolutely, I would.

Dr. Glenn: Can you take a very conservative guess of what that would be worth?

Denise: I'd say $500 a month.

Dr. Glenn: That's $6,000 a year. If we combine those figures, it's more than $1,000 a month and more than $10,000 a year. Do you believe that? Is that figure realistic?

Denise: I absolutely believe it.

Dr. Glenn: Could there be anything in your relationship that would improve?

Denise: I could do more things with my kids that are physical. They're very physical kids. They go outside and they don't like to be in the house very often. They want to be outside playing.

Dr. Glenn: What would you do with them?

Denise: Anything. Go for a walk. Go on the trampoline. We have a park right by us, and we could take the dog out with us. Go on hikes.

Dr. Glenn: Somebody put a battery in them and forgot to take it out. I know kids like that. It's hard for parents sometimes. Would you enjoy more activities with them if you had the energy?

Denise: Yes, I would.

Dr. Glenn: What about with your husband? Will anything change?

Denise: It's the same thing. He likes to go on hikes and do things like that too.

Dr. Glenn: What about your friends?

Denise: It wouldn't be all focused around food. I feel like sometimes that's the focal point of what we're going to do.

Dr. Glenn: What would you do instead?

Denise: I don't know. Just relax.

Dr. Glenn: You might just hang out and relax and talk. Make memories. What else would be different in a year if you did this perfectly?

Denise: I would be able to plan and figure out what I'm going to do next once the kids are in school full time.

Dr. Glenn: Your brain is going to be popping with ideas for a week or so. Try to capture it. It's going to help you.

Denise: Okay. I will.

Dr. Glenn: At this juncture, I remind people that you know I like you, but I don't like your Pig very much. If you feel uncomfortable, it's just the Pig inside you that I'm attacking.

Denise: Right. I know that.

Dr. Glenn: We want to give your Pig a chance. We want it to be able to say all the reasons why we can't or won't do this. So far, we know it says, "You can start tomorrow," "Your family is eating Pig slop and therefore you should be able to eat it too," "It's not fair that you've got to be different," "It's going to take so long to get where you want to go, so why bother?" and "Just another bite won't hurt." What else is the Pig saying?

Denise: That's pretty much everything -- it's on a loop.

Dr. Glenn: You don't want to give it one more chance to say something else?

Denise: No. That's pretty much what it does. It keeps me very much under its control by keeping on that same loop.

Dr. Glenn: Up until this point, it actually thought that it could keep you under control -- for a little while. Obviously, you managed to cage your Pig for some time and lose 20 pounds. That's no small accomplishment. If you did it before, you can do it again. And if you can do it for a month, you can do it for a year.

Let's go through this and jump back up into your higher self. I want to hear what you think a better answer might be, especially in consideration of everything we've just talked about, and then where you need help, I'll help you. You're not going to have to remember these answers, but it's really helpful to do a rational disputation of your Pig's best squeals at least once to expose them to the light of day and see how silly they really are.

Denise: Okay.

Dr. Glenn: When the Pig says, "I'll start tomorrow," what's a better answer to that one? How would you dispute that?

Denise: I'll start right now.

Dr. Glenn: How come?

Denise: Because tomorrow might not come. Tomorrow is not guaranteed.

Dr. Glenn: Now is the only time you can feed yourself, right?

Denise: Right.

Dr. Glenn: What else makes "I'll start tomorrow" not such a great idea?

Denise: Why wait until tomorrow? What's so special about tomorrow?

Dr. Glenn: Do you want me to give you a couple of other things that help people in this situation?

Denise: Yes, please.

Dr. Glenn: The first one you're really saying already. Tomorrow is not guaranteed. We don't have a time machine. The only time that we can feed ourselves is now. The other one is that every time you feed the Pig, you make the craving stronger. It's the principle of neuroplasticity -- that which wires together, fires together. If you have a craving and you feed it, you're training your brain. The pathways in your brain wire together to produce those cravings even more strongly the next day.

The Pig is saying, "I'll start tomorrow -- it doesn't matter one way or the other," but the truth is that every choice has a very serious impact on the level of cravings and how much difficulty you have in resisting them. You can either feed the addiction or starve it. You can either reinforce the addiction or begin to extinguish it. If you eat healthy today, the craving is going to be easier to deal with tomorrow. If you eat healthy tomorrow, the craving is going to be easier to deal with the next day. If you eat badly today, you're going to have a harder time with the craving tomorrow. That's the truth, the unfortunate and fortunate truth, about how our brains are wired.

What about when the Pig says, "My family is eating Pig slop and I should be able to eat it too. It's not fair that I have to be different"?

Denise: It's just a fact that I am different. That is where I am in my life. It goes back to the same thing that you just said. If you feed it, you fire it. If you starve it, you're extinguishing it.

Dr. Glenn: What else? "My family is eating Pig slop and I should be able to eat it too. It's not fair to be different."

Denise: I'm trying to reach a goal, so in order to reach the goal, I have to be different.

Dr. Glenn: Very good. What else?

Denise: I don't know. That's all I got on that one.

Dr. Glenn: There are a couple of things that help people here.

One is the idea that average in our society is really pretty awful. If you look at the incidence of diabetes, cancer, and heart attacks alone, the majority of us are doomed to suffering if we follow the average course that the typical American follows. If you want to be healthy, you have to be different. If you do what everybody else does, you're going to get what everybody else gets. Average is really horrible. I don't want to be average. I don't strive to be average. I strive to be way above average in terms of the way I take care of my health. The majority of people in our society make all kinds of excuses to kill themselves slowly.

And when I'm with people that I love, I want to be a healthy leader. I find that explaining to them why this or that food is better for them doesn't work so well, but when they look at the fact that my skin is clear, I lost 60 pounds, I have all this energy, and I'm accomplishing all these things, then they start to get curious about what am I doing differently.

What do you think when the Pig says, "It's going to take you so long to get where you want to be, so why bother?"

Denise: I'm going to end up being there anyhow. Even if it takes a year, the year is going to come and go whether I want it or not, so I might as well accomplish something. You can either live the year peacefully or chaotically.

Dr. Glenn: In misery.

Denise: In misery, yes.

Dr. Glenn: Because the Pig is really taking away your enjoyment of life. You can't be yourself at all when the Pig is out of its cage.

Denise: No.

Dr. Glenn: Am I exaggerating?

Denise: No, not at all. That's right on point.

Dr. Glenn: What about when the Pig says, "Just one bite won't hurt"?

Denise: That's crazy. It goes back to your never, always, and any sort of exceptions. Whatever is on that list, that's what you've got to stick with.

Dr. Glenn: You can change the plan if you want to. If everything is too strict, you can change it.

Denise: You can change it, but I know what's going to keep me on track and what isn't, and one bite will make all the difference. It feeds the obsession.

Dr. Glenn: And what's the point of defining a target if you're not going to aim for it? One bite could actually be a catastrophe. If you give the Pig an inch, it'll take a mile.

Denise: Yes, because I envision the Pig as big or small. This makes it really big, and then it's not in its cage.

Dr. Glenn: That's why I really like your jewelry, which has a little small Pig in the cage, where it's very easy to control.

Denise: You can control it when it's that way. You can't when it gets humungous like the one in the first session that is like the devil and has a pitchfork.

Dr. Glenn: It feels very big, like when a cat puffs up its back. But it's still just a kitty cat. Well, the Pig is a dangerous cat. It's more like a feral cat, but you can still put it in the cage. What about when the Pig says, "Why bother?"

Denise: Because you have to bother. That's a lame thing to say anyhow. As we're going through these things and I feel like I'm gaining more control, my answer is that's just lame. It's not true.

Dr. Glenn: That's what happens when you expose the Pig to the light of day. It just wants to indulge and it doesn't really care about your goals and dreams. "Why bother?" is the Pig's mantra.

The Pig is getting at you by saying, "Why bother?" I think the answer is, "Because I'm important and I want to be able to live my life."

How confident do you feel that you're never going to binge again?

Denise: 150 percent. It's like I just needed a refresher.

Dr. Glenn: Sometimes that's all people need. Sometimes it's all I need.

Denise: I may joke, but it's really been on a loop. I just needed something to break the loop.

Dr. Glenn: Is your Pig having a knee-jerk reaction to the 150 percent? Do you hear anything in the background?

Denise: No, because it's really small and back in its cage.

Dr. Glenn: What would you say to people who are procrastinating about caging their Pig after having gone through this exercise?

Denise: It will really be okay once you cage your Pig. There's hope. You just have to take that first step.

Dr. Glenn: It might feel like you're drowning in the mud, but you just have to stand up.

Denise: That's exactly it. You just have stand strong and move forward. Put one foot in front of the other.

CHAPTER 2: CAN THE PIG KNOCK YOU UNCONSCIOUS AND MAKE YOU BINGE?

Introduction

Just how powerful IS the Pig?

Can it knock you unconscious, take full control of your arms, hands, finger, mouth, teeth, tongue, and throat and force you to eat Pig Slop? Can the Pig MAKE you Binge?

You'd think this was the case when you talk to some people about their experience after a Binge... In fact MOST people feel like this at some point if they genuinely struggle with overeating. But is it really true?

Interview Audio

https://www.neverbingeagain.com/TheBlog/recorded-sessions/
can-the-pig-knock-you-unconscious-and-make-you-binge/

What to watch for in this interview:

- How the feeling of powerlessness over food is really a Pig Squeal and what to do to overcome it

- Why you can succeed even if you've failed countless times before

- How to avoid binge eating even when you have really bad days

Interview begins here

Dr. Glenn: Howard Jacobson from plantyourself.com asked if I would listen to a 15-minute coaching call he had with a client. So, what happened with Ethel?

Howie: Ethel had been doing well and then stopped doing well. This is something that scares me a little bit as a coach because everything that had been working all of a sudden stopped working. We were working largely off the Never Binge Again model, as incorporated into the coaching program that I offer around exercise and plant-based nutrition. Out of the blue, it stopped working. I wanted to explore with her so that we had a clear sense of what had happened, why it had happened and what we could do about it next time. I started feeling anxious that I was going to be helpless.

Dr. Glenn: And what happened?

Howie: I felt very good after the call. I felt like we had explored. The revelation that people come to again and again -- "Oh, that was the Pig" -- never ceases to amaze me. We got to that point. And yet I wasn't sure from the conversation whether I had manufactured the moment because I was so desperately looking for an objective answer, or whether we had actually stumbled upon objective reality. That's mostly what I wanted help with, but also how I introduced the question, how I led her through it, and whether my questions empowered or disempowered her.

Dr. Glenn: I think I can help you with your anxiety. The cause of your anxiety is actually based on a mistaken assumption. We're going to shift your paradigm just a little bit. The assumption you have is that Never Binge Again is like a gastric bypass that makes it impossible for people to make the wrong choice anymore. That's not really what it is. Never Binge Again is a methodology for restoring your sense of free will and control over what you put in your mouth.

Once you get that free will and control, there are two things that can cause you to put Pig slop into your mouth. One of them is you, and the other is the Pig. The Pig can do it if it manages to fool you into thinking its squeals are actually your own thoughts. What typically happens is people learn the methodology and then the Pig starts working really hard to come up with a squeal that you won't recognize or it finds a hole in your food plan.

The people that get it just get up again. They figure out how can they recognize what Pig squeal got by them and if they need to change anything in their food plan to make sure it can't get by them again. Was it just a simple Pig attack that we're going to ignore now?

The Pig can get you to put food in your mouth only if it fools you into thinking the thoughts are yours. The sense of relief that people have after the coaching session is that they recognize where the Pig got by them. But you can also choose to put something in your mouth that's not on your food plan. I can't take away your free will. I can point out to you all of the illusions that prevent you from believing that you do have free will. I can take away the sense of powerlessness. I can give you a sense of hope that it really is possible to never binge again, but I can't take away your free will.

In those situations, you just have to help people reorient themselves. Eventually, they start saying, "I reached in and I opened the Pig's cage. I wanted to." And that's not nearly as frightening or overwhelming an experience as feeling out of control. People know that if they opened up the Pig's cage, they can lock it up again. Eventually, they get sick of letting the Pig out. It's just not worth it.

I know people don't believe me, but underneath a craving for chocolate is possibly a craving for broccoli. The more you have the experience of letting the survival drive do what it's supposed to do as opposed to the industrial food, the less you really want the industrial food. The trick is to figure out what happened. How did the Pig sneak something by you? How did you reverse your intent and choose to open up the cage, and what do you want to do about it?

It's not your responsibility as a coach to stop her from binging. That's not possible. All that's possible is for you to really clarify where her free will is, what her choices are and what the Pig said that she didn't recognize.

Howie: Can I share something about a different person who just posted something? This is totally anonymous, and I'll change the details as well. "The last week has been one raging, eternal battle. It's like a dark cloud just parks over me and it's there. I just do things that are bad for me." The person goes into several examples. "The only self-thought that stands out is the part of me that's so judgmental and disappointed. I identify the Pig and I know what it is, but it's like I have no control over it sometimes. Sometimes I do. This is what I don't understand. I can go weeks and weeks without this happening and all of a sudden, boom, it happens. I end up feeling physically and emotionally bad, and I don't lose weight this way."

        I don't coach this person one-on-one. This is just someone who is part of the group. But I'm sure that happens to people and I'll get that situation. For this person, it feels like they're walking and then lightning strikes. They have no control over it. They know everything, but the only thing they can do is feel bad and blame themselves.

Dr. Glenn: So, role play this with me. You take on the role of the person who's feeling powerless. Hey, it's Glenn from Never

Binge Again. How are you?

Howie: I'm good.

Dr. Glenn: Good. What can I do for you today?

Howie: I know all about the Pig. I read the book twice. It all makes sense, so I can go weeks following the Never Binge Again model, but then all of a sudden I'll do these things that I know are not in my best interest and I'll feel terrible about it. I can't stop myself.

Dr. Glenn: What food plan are you trying to follow? What are the rules you're trying to follow?

Howie: Plant-based, no extra oil, no added sugar, whole food.

Dr. Glenn: How do you define sugar?

Howie: Added sugar to things.

Dr. Glenn: What does that mean?

Howie: It's dessert food, candy, cakes and donuts. I'm not confused about what's on the plan. When I'm doing the wrong thing, there's no part of me that's fooling myself.

Dr. Glenn: I see. What's happening at the moment you choose to do the wrong thing?

Howie: There's this constant battle going on, and I'm fighting it. I can win, but when the dark cloud comes over, I'm just not strong enough and I lose.

Dr. Glenn: The Pig says it's stronger than you and you're always going to lose. It's got you convinced. It's a subtle shift in language, but do you understand the difference?

Howie: Yes. Instead of me saying, "Here's what happens," I'm saying, "The Pig has convinced me that this is what happens."

Dr. Glenn: And why is that important?

Howie: Because if it's what happens, then it's my script. It's the story that I'm going to live and there's no way out of it. But if I say this is just the story that the Pig has told me that opens up to possibility that it's not true.

Dr. Glenn: What do you want to do about this?

Howie: I want to take control, so I don't end up feeling physically and emotionally bad and stop my weight loss. It discourages me about all the good stuff that came before. It's like all of that has been wiped away. It doesn't exist anymore.

Dr. Glenn: Your Pig says the moment you make a mistake, everything you've accomplished is ruined and you might as well just give up.

Howie: Yes.

Dr. Glenn: Why does your Pig say that?

Howie: Because it wants me to give up.

Dr. Glenn: How come?

Howie: Because then the Pig gets what it wants. It gets to binge.

Dr. Glenn: Right. Do you think that anyone has ever had a major accomplishment where they didn't make tons of mistakes along the way? Where they didn't fall back down the mountain a whole bunch of times?

Howie: No, probably not.

Dr. Glenn: Then it's actually a sign of strength that you keep getting up to try again, right?

Howie: It could be a sign of stupidity if it's not the path that I should be taking.

Dr. Glenn: The Pig says it is a sign of stupidity and you're not smart enough to figure out how to stop binging. What do you want to do about this?

Howie: I want to get control over it, but I don't want to be disappointed again. I'm almost scared to try again.

Dr. Glenn: The Pig says you're going to feel so demoralized if you make another mistake that you might as well not even try.

Howie: Yes.

Dr. Glenn: And the Pig wants you to make a plan to forget. The Pig is planning for you to screw up, but the essence of a vow is a plan to remember. You didn't necessarily make a solid vow last time. You made a wishy-washy Piggy vow, where the Pig was telling you that you were going to forget the whole time. What do you want to do about this?

Howie: I want to remember the vow and stick to it.

Dr. Glenn: Why can't you do that?

Howie: I need a way to deal with that dark cloud.

Dr. Glenn: Why can't you have a dark cloud over your head and not binge?

Howie: I don't know.

Dr. Glenn: Do you have to binge if you have a dark cloud over your head? Could you just have a bad day?

Howie: That's what I want. I want to not have to binge.

Dr. Glenn: The next time you have a bad day, are you going to binge?

Howie: History is saying yes.

Dr. Glenn: So, you're planning to then?

Howie: I'll see.

Dr. Glenn: Behind every fear is a wish. Behind the fear you're going to binge is the Pig's plan to binge.

I'm separating this person from their Pig. Every question is driving them further and further apart. It makes them uncomfortable, but it's really the Pig's feelings that are uncomfortable.

Howie: Yes, I see.

Dr. Glenn: I just keep on driving them apart until they don't have any more excuses and they say, "It just feels like I'm going to." I say, "That's because you have a Pig inside. It's always going to want to binge. You're always going to feel that, but you don't ever have to do it again." Does that make sense?

Howie: Yes.

Dr. Glenn: People make mistakes. You help them and they get back up.

Howie: When you listened to my session, was there anything that you thought I could have done better?

Dr. Glenn: Actually, I thought you were a very talented coach. You ask some questions and did some things in ways that I learned from. I did sense your feeling of responsibility for the client's choice. I did sense your panic. After our talk today, I think you'll be more comfortable and understand that you're really just trying to separate the client from their Pig and give them back a sense of free will. Some clients will choose to binge, but you're not going to let them have the excuse that they're powerless.

Howie: It feels very important to not take responsibility for them.

Dr. Glenn: I was very gentle, but direct. I just kept on separating you from the Pig. Every time you tried to convince me that it was you, I kept on attributing the doubt to the Pig until you couldn't use that excuse anymore.

Howie: And you were also very comfortable with my discomfort.

Dr. Glenn: Yes.

Howie: That told me that you were holding a container for my discomfort and I didn't owe you anything. This was all for me.

Dr. Glenn: It was absolutely your choice what you wanted to do.

Howie: That's very helpful.

CHAPTER 3: SEPARATING YOUR THOUGHTS FROM THE PIG'S THOUGHTS

Introduction

Ever feel totally confused about what the Pig is saying vs. what YOU genuinely believe? In this interview you'll hear Denise struggle to separate her thoughts from the Pig's... until she realizes its plain as day! (The beginning of the interview is a little slow while she is confused – but it's very worth reading in order to thoroughly understand how your Pig will try to confuse the issue, and how utterly simple it is to hear the Pig once you "get it")

Interview Audio

https://www.neverbingeagain.com/TheBlog/recorded-sessions/separating-your-thoughts-from-the-pigs-thoughts/

What to watch for in this interview

- How Denise's Pig introduced a Trojan horse into her eating plan – so you can avoid your Pig's attempts to do the same

- How to deal with the "Let's start with the diet tomorrow" pig squeals

- What exactly to think about our eating failures in order to stop them fast

· How to deal with the fear of failing

Interview Begins Here

Dr. Glenn: How are things going?

Denise: I am still struggling with my inability to realize this is a long process and taking off the weight is not going to happen overnight. I'm afraid this isn't going to work, and if that's the case, what else is out there for me. Trying to plan everything is so overwhelming for me.

About 10 years ago, I would not eat enough. I was very thin. Because I was restricting my food, I started to binge, which got me to where I am now. I go back and forth in my head, and I'm sure it's the Pig talking. "Maybe you should starve yourself again. That served you well so many years ago." I'm not eating enough, and I'm so hungry that no plan will work.

Dr. Glenn: The specific squeals that are getting to you are, "You can start tomorrow," "This little bit is not going to hurt," and "It's going to take a very long time to take this off. It's just too big a mountain, so let's not even start climbing." And you said you're afraid it's not going to work. Could you tell me a little bit more about that? Why wouldn't it work?

Denise: The Pig is just saying, "This isn't going to work, so why bother trying?"

Dr. Glenn: "Nothing is going to work for you. You're going through silly efforts. You should just accept being a happy fat person."

Denise: Yes.

Dr. Glenn: Do you believe that there really is nothing that will work for you?

Denise: On an intellectual level, I don't believe that. When I think about the Pig and I bash the squeals, I don't believe that. But I'm in a circle that I need to break out of. If I stick to my plan, don't listen to the squeals and don't feed the fire, then it will work.

Dr. Glenn: What's stopping you from breaking out of the circle?

Denise: I'm listening to the squeals, I guess.

Dr. Glenn: The Pig says, "Let's start tomorrow." How do you dispute that?

Denise: Before I listen to the squeal, I have to go for a 30-minute walk or even just a walk around the block. If after my walk I still believe the Pig, then I can have at it. Usually what ends up happening is I don't want to listen to the squeal. Walking starts to extinguish the fire.

Dr. Glenn: Is your food plan written in such a way that if you walk for 30 minutes the other rules are no longer valid?

Denise: No, I don't think so.

Dr. Glenn: I support the idea that you should walk for 30 minutes if the Pig is bothering you, but I'm a little concerned that it might be inserting a kind of Trojan Horse. It says, "I'll give you these 30 minutes, but if I still feel like eating after that, then you've got to feed me."

Denise: It's a different way of giving in.

Dr. Glenn: Yes. Your plan is your plan. If you want your plan to say you can have anything you want after walking for 30 minutes, I'm open to talking about that possibility.

Denise: No, I don't want to do that. I just need to not listen to the Pig, and I think what it ends up coming down to is that all these things I wrote down are just BS.

Dr. Glenn: I'd like to look at the squeals more specifically be-cause you're finding them convincing. One of the ways the Pig was convincing you was by giving you this Trojan Horse. " I'll let you walk for 30 minutes, but if I still feel like eating, then I get to go to town." We have to step back and say that's just not how it is. You make the laws. You say, "I'm going to walk for 30 minutes so I feel more comfortable, but you stay in the cage no matter what."

How else would you dispute the Pig when it says, "Let's start tomorrow"?

Denise: That you're not even guaranteed a tomorrow. I have to keep the Pig in its cage and say, "Let's start right now."

Dr. Glenn: There is no tomorrow.

Denise: There's only right now.

Dr. Glenn: The only time you can eat healthy is now.

Denise: I just have to put a double lock on the cage right now.

Dr. Glenn: You know if you give in to the Pig today, it's going to be harder to resist tomorrow. And you know that if you keep the Pig in the cage today, then it's easier to keep the Pig in the cage tomorrow.

Denise: I don't know why I'm fighting it so hard some days. I think my food plan possibly has too many holes in it. I'm giving myself outs. I'm giving myself permission to let the Pig out of its cage.

Dr. Glenn: Where are the holes?

Denise: I'm not relying on my nevers and always. I started to get cocky, and I'm not relying on the basic tools. There are a lot of holes in what I'm doing right now. For me, I don't know that I can ever have holes in my plan that are going to let the Pig get out of its cage.

Dr. Glenn: I'm not sure if there are holes in the food plan itself, or if the Pig is squealing about exceptions and you're listening to it.

Denise: I think that's what I'm doing. If I go to a restaurant, I can have 10 tortilla chips. But I think I can never have tortilla chips, and I'm letting the Pig give me exceptions.

Dr. Glenn: What are the exceptions that the Pig is giving you that you need to eliminate in your food plan?

Denise: Basically, the Pig cannot come out. I have to really follow my Nevers and Always. I made up little cards for myself with all my Nevers and Always. I need to just work the program and not listen to the exceptions. I haven't realized that these have been Pig squeals. I've look at them more as me failing.

Dr. Glenn: That's how the Pig wants you to see it. The Pig doesn't want you to separate from it. It wants you to think you are a failure and you're too weak to resist. To clarify, your food plan says you'll never eat tortillas?

Denise: Yes. I don't eat flour. I can't really handle sugar.

Dr. Glenn: You can't really handle it or you never eat it? What does it actually say in black and white?

Denise: I never eat it because my body doesn't handle processed foods well.

Dr. Glenn: Your food plan says you'll never eat flour or sugar?

Denise: Right.

Dr. Glenn: Therefore, any thought whatsoever that says you could have a few tortilla chips in the restaurant or after a 30-minute walk has got to be a Pig squeal.

Denise: Yes.

Dr. Glenn: I'm sorry if this feels a little uncomfortable. We're attacking your Pig now.

Denise: I know you're not attacking me. I know it's the Pig. The Pig has overtaken me. I didn't realize they were squeals.

Dr. Glenn: You do know they're squeals.

Denise: I do now.

Dr. Glenn: The Pig wants to keep you in a state of confusion. It doesn't want you to recognize these things, but it's really clear that you don't have flour or sugar in your food plan. When you hear in your head, "Flour or sugar is okay in any circumstance whatsoever between now and the day that you die," that's a squeal. It doesn't matter how rational it sounds at the moment.

Denise: Instead of the 30-minute walk, I might try to write down all these things and recognize them as squeals. Write them down and recognizing them as squeals would get them out of my head. It might break me out of that loop.

Dr. Glenn: It will help if you see it on paper. This is a perfect example of the Pig convincing someone that it doesn't really exist and the squeals are their own thinking. This is a perfect example of the confusion between the self and the Pig. That's the Pig's strategy right now.

Denise: I was doing so well, but I let it come back in and confuse me.

Dr. Glenn: Let's talk more specifically about the squeals you mentioned. You said the Pig says weight loss is a long process, so you might as well not bother. Could you tell me a little bit more about that?

Denise: I know I have a long way to go. I say, "In a year, can you imagine where you'll be?" And then my Pig comes out and says, "You've already tried for a year. What if you would have tried before? You wouldn't be where you are right now." I think that's what is happening. " I've already failed. Why keep going?" That's my big Pig squeal.

Dr. Glenn: You know that winners keep getting up until they win.

Denise: Yes.

Dr. Glenn: Are you confident in your ability to recognize that squeal, or is there something else going on your head that is going to make it difficult to ignore?

Denise: No, I don't think so. I've got to write it down and recognize it as a squeal. It's playing on this loop. It's the same stuff playing over and over again, and I just thought it was me, not the squeal. Even though I knew it, like you said.

Dr. Glenn: Between now and the time you write it down, are you going to be able to recognize a voice in your head that says, "Weight loss takes too long. You might as well binge"? Are you going to be able to recognize that is a squeal?

Denise: I have to recognize that whatever I'm thinking, I've got to give myself a minute or two before I let it overtake me. It will be hard at first, but I think that's what I have to do.

Dr. Glenn: If there's a voice in your head saying you should eat sugar or flour even if there's no sugar or flour in your food plan, how difficult is it to recognize that would be the Pig?

Denise: It's not difficult now that I've talked it through and clarified it. I'm making very affirmative statements, whereas over the past week I allowed myself to be very wishy-washy. That's been the Pig.

Dr. Glenn: The Pig wants to keep you in a state of confusion and fear. That way you can't really decide whether or not you're abstaining from something and you're frightened of being near Pig slop. The Pig will tell you it's a foregone conclusion that you have to binge. But the bottom line is you don't eat sugar and flour. That's just who you are. We can recognize that as a squeal right away.

How would you dispute the Pig when it says, "This can't work. It's going to be one more thing that doesn't work"?

Denise: I would just turn it into an affirmative statement. It will work.

Dr. Glenn: Will you accomplish your physical goals if you don't eat sugar and flour?

Denise: Yes.

Dr. Glenn: How could it not work if you recognize all of the nonsense that the Pig is throwing at you and ignore it?

Denise: It will work.

Dr. Glenn: Is there any way that it could not work?

Denise: I don't see any reason why it wouldn't work.

Dr. Glenn: I don't see any reason why it wouldn't work either. There's an interesting thing about psychological fears. Behind every fear is usually a wish. When you hear in your head that you're afraid this isn't going to work, what you want to do is translate it: "The Pig really hopes this won't work. It wants to sabotage us, but I'm in control." You want to switch that language because the natural extension is to say, " I'm in control, so it is going to work." "I'm afraid it's not going to work" is the Pig saying, "I really want this to fail." Does that make sense?

Denise: Yes, it does. When the thought comes into my head, besides writing it down I should turn it into, "That's what the Pig wants me to think."

Dr. Glenn: What about the idea that planning is overwhelming? How would you dispute that?

Denise: Planning is necessary to keep the Pig away.

Dr. Glenn: How much planning do you need to do to work that out?

Denise: Once I get into what it's going to look like, it's not going to be difficult at all. I have to plan.

Dr. Glenn: In the planning you're doing, can you create some default meals that you can go to in a contingency if for some reason you don't have a specific plan for the day?

Denise: That's a good idea. I'll do that.

Dr. Glenn: What's a better answer for when the Pig says you should starve yourself so you can lose weight faster like you did last time?

Denise: I absolutely cannot do that. There's no way that will work.

Dr. Glenn: The antidote is a normal, healthy diet without sugar and flour. That's the antidote to your problem. Do you believe that?

Denise: Yes, I believe that.

Dr. Glenn: I'm going for your Pig's jugular because you've been having a hard time. The Pig really got you confused. I'm trying to make the Pig squirm. I'm trying to expose every last little trick it's throwing at you.

Denise: I think you have done that.

Dr. Glenn: Are you feeling confident?

Denise: I have to keep saying I will succeed if I stay away from flour and sugar and have a reasonable diet that meets all my needs.

Dr. Glenn: I'm not sure I hear it in your voice. Is there something going on in the back of your head that's bothering you about this?

Denise: No, I have to do it. I don't have a choice anymore. I have to stay away from flour and sugar starting right this second in order to meet my goals.

Dr. Glenn: You've already been away from it for half an hour, unless you've been eating on the call.

Denise: No, I haven't been eating on the call..

Dr. Glenn: So, you've already been away from flour and sugar for half an hour.

Denise: Right. I have to keep on the same track. I cannot eat flour and sugar in order to succeed, and I want to succeed.

Dr. Glenn: Will you or won't you?

Denise: I will. I'm going to get rid of the Pig squeals. I'm not going to just keep them quiet. I'm going to get rid of them.

Dr. Glenn: How confident are you that you'll never eat flour or sugar again between now and the day that you die?

Denise: I am 150 percent confident.

Dr. Glenn: Even if your Pig has other ideas?

Denise: Even if my Pig has other ideas. If a Pig squeal comes up, I'm going to chant that I will never have flour and sugar again in order to meet my goals. That's why I'm doing it.

Dr. Glenn: There will be a lot of new things in your head to start. The Pig is not going to give up, but all you have to do is never have flour and sugar again. No more of these crazy reasons for exceptions.

Denise: I'll just confidently keep saying I can never have flour and sugar again.

Dr. Glenn: What's wrong with that?

Denise: What's wrong with never having flour and sugar again? Nothing.

Dr. Glenn: Did your doctor tell you you're not eating enough flour and sugar?

Denise: No.

Dr. Glenn: Is there some nutritional component of flour and sugar that you're frightened you won't get if you don't eat it again?

Denise: Absolutely not.

Dr. Glenn: Do you feel the need to spend money on flour and sugar that you're not spending elsewhere?

Denise: Nope.

Dr. Glenn: Will it upset you if you start slowly losing weight and heading towards your goal?

Denise: No.

Dr. Glenn: Isn't it joyful when you get the Pig out of the way?

Denise: It is. It's very joyful.

CHAPTER 4: GETTING BACK ON TRACK (AGAIN)

Introduction

Do you know what's harder than getting back on track after a Binge? NOT getting back on track!

Interview Audio

https://www.neverbingeagain.com/TheBlog/food-rules/getting-back-on-track-again/

Things to watch for in this interview

- How lose-weight-fast diets actually work with your Pig to make sure that you never do lose any weight

- How to harness past successes to create a powerful force that will allow you to lock away your pig forever

- How to break the effect your parents (specifically your mother) have on your eating

Interview Begins Here

Dr. Glenn: Alexandria did really well for a while after her last session, but she had some serious trouble, which is not unusual. People can lose it and they need a little help getting back. What happened?

Alexandria: We had spoken on a Saturday. On Sunday, I was going to a family party, so I said I'm not going to do anything today. I'm going to start Monday. On Monday morning, I started on the food plan that I had chosen, which was Whole30. I had done it previously and felt really great on it. And it lasted about five days. I felt really in control and empowered until I stepped on the scale and saw I'd only lost four pounds in five days, and everything went to hell. I felt so discouraged.

It completely set my mind back. All of a sudden, I started thinking maybe this isn't the right plan. I started cycling through diets again and I lost a month because I read the book and re-listened to my session. I listened to some of your other interviews and videos, but I was never able to fully get a hold of myself again. This week, I decided I was going to start something brand new that I hadn't done before. I was mentally prepared, and I went through a drive-through to get my coffee and ended up getting donuts and eating them. Where the heck did that come from? I said I'm ready to do this and I couldn't even make it 10 minutes.

Dr. Glenn: You got derailed by this notion that four pounds in five days is horrible. How much did you think you should have lost in five days?

Alexandria: I don't know. Some plans say you could lose eight or nine pounds in a week.

Dr. Glenn: That's dangerous. I don't mean to be judgmental, but --

Alexandria: I know. I need to stay off the scale. That needs to be a hard and fast rule with me because I have issues with weighing myself. I get very discouraged, even if the results are obviously good. Looking back, somebody else would be absolutely thrilled with that number, but I need to stay off the scale because it just causes me too much mental anguish. I become paralyzed, and then I get all the doubts and I start jumping around again. I lose time.

Dr. Glenn: What do you think is realistic to lose each week?

Alexandria: Two or three pounds, if you're going to be consistent. The first week or two would be a little bit better -- not necessarily nine or 10 pounds, but maybe four or five pounds because you lose a little bit more water during at first. After that, you consistently lose maybe two or three pounds a weeks.

Dr. Glenn: Do you have more than 100 pounds to lose?

Alexandria: I have about 80.

Dr. Glenn: I worked with a guy that started at 500 pounds. What finally worked for him was deciding to lose five pounds a month. He said, "It took me a long time to get here. I built myself this fat prison, and I just have to do some time here to get out." I know it's not what people want to hear. They want the weight off really quickly. And in the beginning, it might come off a little quicker, but I find that the clients losing more than two pounds a week bounce back.

I try to guide people to have an expectation of no more than a pound or two a week, or around five pounds a month. If you can do that consistently rather than jumping from diet to diet and panicking that it's not working, then it's going to be a little more than a year before you get it all off.

Alexandria: That sounds like absolute torture to me. But years go by and I haven't lost the weight. I've been struggling with this consistently for a couple of years. If I had started a year ago and lost a pound a week, I'd be where I want to be right now. But because I have these expectations and jump around between diets, I just never get anywhere.

Dr. Glenn: If you're engaged in a diet plan that's supposed to have you losing eight pounds in a week, you're very likely triggering an evolutionary mechanism that says, "This person is going through starvation, and as soon as calories are available, I better hoard them." You're feeding into the binge. I'm usually not quite this directive. I'm usually more interested in exactly what your Pig is saying. I was just a little shocked you thought it was not enough to lose four pounds in five days because most of my clients would think that was terrific.

Alexandria: If a friend had told me they lost four pounds in the last five days, I would say, "That's great. You must be really watching what you're eating because that's a really good loss." When it comes to myself, I just hear all this noise in my head: I'm not good enough, it should have been more, you have to do something different, you're never going to do it anyway. It gets really loud and confusing until I feel I'm paralyzed and I end up eating junk. It's a vicious cycle.

Dr. Glenn: Tell me more about the noise in your head. What else goes on in your head at those times?

Alexandria: It's a little painful to talk about. My mom passed away two years ago. She was a lifelong smoker, even though she was sick and had quadruple bypass heart surgery and high blood pressure. When she got out of the hospital after finding out that she had cancer and was in kidney failure, the first thing she did was grab a cigarette and start smoking.

She never really spoke to me much about it. She did make attempts throughout her life to quit at certain points. With her it was cigarettes and with me it was food. She was never able to quit smoking. I'm never going to be able to stop eating and I'll never be able to get a hold of this.

Dr. Glenn: My mom has a serious recurrence of ovarian cancer. She's going through very aggressive chemotherapy, and I went to stay with her for a couple of weeks to help her out. I thought when I got there I would find her eating greens and juices and have fruits and vegetables all over the house. Instead, she was eating pizza and bagels. I love my mom and she's not going to change now, but I had a sinking feeling. At that moment, the Pig told me, "The apple doesn't fall far from the tree. If she can't do it, then you can't do it." But I have done it, and I am going to do it for the rest of my life. My mother had a different childhood than I did. She was raised during a different era. She actually wants me to be healthy, and she's happy for me when I eat healthy.

She bought me all kinds of bananas, pears and greens. She wanted to make sure I was happy and that I was not eating the stuff she was eating. It's helpful sometimes to step back and say you wish your parents were different. I love my mom. I really wish she was different, but she has her life and I have mine.

You love your mom and you really connected to her. This is an important pattern that your Pig has internalized without you knowing about it, so it's important that you talk about it.

Alexandria: She died in 2015. I was 41.

Dr. Glenn: It's normal when we really miss someone to want to be like them. It's our way of having them with us.

We could think about whether there was anything positive that you could emulate about your mom to keep her with you rather than emulating her smoking or her self-destruction.

Alexandria: My mom was tough. She was a single mother with six girls, and she was a tough woman. I respect that she'd always do what she had to do. I'm like that too, in that way. I'm always just charging ahead. I just figure out a way. If this thing isn't working, we'll find a different way to do it. I respect and admire that about her.

Dr. Glenn: When the Pig says, "We should just give up and binge," does that reflect this character trait that your mom gave you?

Alexandria: No, not at all.

Dr. Glenn: What would your mom say if she heard your Pig talking like that?

Alexandria: My mom could curse a blue streak. She'd say, "Shut the F*%$ up." She would tell me I'm being an idiot. Just figure this out. She wouldn't even take it seriously. She'd say, " Get over your pity-party. Move on. "

Dr. Glenn: Would she tell you to do the Whole30 Plan if that's what's going to work for you or would she tell you to do something else?

Alexandria: She would tell me to do what would work for me. She'd tell me to do whatever would make me feel good. "If that thing is going to work, then shut up and do it."

Dr. Glenn: Do you still believe that Whole30 is your best guess for a food plan going forward?

Alexandria: I've done a million diets in my life. When I was on this plan, I had a feeling of such good health. I felt healthy and positive, and I keep trying to get that back. Even when I only do it for a couple of days, I see the changes starting to happen. I start feeling better, and I don't feel that way when I do any of these other plans. I don't feel as good when I eliminate all carbs and load up on fats, or I eat low-fat. I felt good on Whole30 and I just want that back.

Dr. Glenn: Why can't the last bite of Pig slop that you had today be the last one that you take? Why can't you do that forever, or at least until you have the weight off?

Alexandria: I just feel like I'm going to screw it up.

Dr. Glenn: Why?

Alexandria: Because I won't be able to say no. I won't be able to stop.

Dr. Glenn: Is that you or your Pig talking?

Alexandria: It's the Pig. It's just all those negative thoughts. It's not really me.

Dr. Glenn: I have the impression you're a strong woman.

Alexandria: I am. That's how I see myself.

Dr. Glenn: I have the impression you don't take much crap actually.

Alexandria: No, not really.

Dr. Glenn: But sometimes when the Pig talks, you're willing to take his crap.

Alexandria: Yes.

Dr. Glenn: What are we going to do about that?

Alexandria: I need to work really hard on recognizing that it's not me. When I say, "I am never going to eat wheat, sugar and dairy again," and it says, "Yeah, right," I realize that's not me.

Dr. Glenn: If you hear a voice that says you should have some wheat, sugar or dairy or that you're not capable of quitting it, isn't that, by definition, the Pig?

Alexandria: It's the Pig because that falls outside of my food plan and what I'm determined to do. That's really just the Pig talking.

Dr. Glenn: What is the Pig saying that you still find believable?

Alexandria: That I'm not going to be able to do it. One thing with a plan like the Whole30 is that maybe I'll eat rice or corn again. It eliminates everything and then eventually you add stuff back in. I really can do without dairy and sugar, but someday I may eat hummus again. I think that causes some confusion in me. I'm never going to eat these things again, but then in the back of my mind, I know I probably will eat some of them again at some point.

Dr. Glenn: Does the Whole30 Plan suggest you add back in the corn, hummus and grains later on?

Alexandria: You eliminate all these foods and you just eat whole, unprocessed healthy foods for a period of time, and then you try to reintroduce some foods and see how you do. Today I'll try rice and see if it feels good. If it doesn't feel good, then you just keep it out of your diet. So, some things I think I probably will eat again at some point when I have a better handle on myself and I've completed the detox portion of the diet.

Dr. Glenn: How long is that supposed to last?

Alexandria: Some people do Whole365. Some people do Whole90. A lot of people just do Whole30. It depends on you. You could do live that way for the rest of your life and never go off of it. It's a completely healthy and sound eating plan.

Dr. Glenn: If you jump into your higher self, what do you think is best for you?

Alexandria: I originally said I would do it for 90 days, but I wrote up a food plan today that says I will never eat wheat, dairy and sugar again for the rest of my life until the day I die. Then I wrote I will do Whole30 and eat just like meat, fats and vegetables. And I wrote that I cannot change my food plan for 30 days.

At the end of 30 days, I'll look at it again. I was listening to what you said in some of your podcasts about giving yourself time. You have to give yourself 24 or 48 hours so you're not impulsive and just changing your food plan to eat what you want in that moment. If I say I cannot change my food plan for 30 days, then at the end of the 30 days I can see if I'll add rice back in.

Dr. Glenn: What's wrong with that?

Alexandria: There's nothing wrong with that. I'm just trying to figure out a way to get rid of the ambiguity. At the end of the 30 days, I can look at it again and decide that maybe I can make these changes at this point. I have time to feel better and have my head clearer. My decisions in 30 days will be different than my decisions today. The way I feel right now, I'm going to feel much different if I consistently stay with it for 30 days.

Dr. Glenn: This sounds like a plan to me.

Alexandria: I think it could work. That wasn't a gung-ho resounding yes.

Dr. Glenn: Your Pig doesn't want you to be confident.

Alexandria: The Pig is saying, "Go away, Glenn."

Dr. Glenn: Your Pig is trying to get rid of me.

Alexandria: We're going to start having technical difficulties. My Pig is going to get my phone.

Dr. Glenn: Your Pig was at it. All doubt and insecurity comes from the Pig. "Yeah, this could work," is a Pig statement. When you declare that this is going to work 100 percent, that's your statement. Don't wait until you feel it. Declare it.

Alexandria: This is what I'm doing and this is going to work. I'm going to make it work. Language is power. I'm going to make it happen.

Dr. Glenn: There's something else. You probably haven't heard me talk about this. The observation that you keep screwing up is actually Pig squeal in and of itself. The Pig wants to collect evidence of failure, but we want to collect evidence of success. When your Pig focuses on all the times you screwed up, it's defining your identity as a failure. But we don't have to do that. We can collect evidence of success. We can go back and look at those five days and figure out what went right. We can think about how you were able to call upon your mom's no-nonsense attitude. We can choose to become a different person even if we've been a screw-up our whole lives. Right now, you've been binge-free for 35 minutes, right?

Alexandria: A whole 35 minutes.

Dr. Glenn: Realistically, you could have had a bag of Cheetos with you this whole time and be putting me on mute while I was talking.

Alexandria: That's absolutely true. Or I could have picked a quieter food that you wouldn't have heard.

Dr. Glenn: For 35 minutes, you've actually been successful. You wanted to do this. You asked me for this session. You came back to me twice. You have that constructive part of you. You're capable of doing this. See, that's collecting evidence of success. When the Pig starts attacking you about the past and what's going to happen in the future, you really have to start with right now. You really have to start with collecting evidence of success right now. There is no food on my mouth this very moment. I am not binging at this very moment.

Alexandria: My son has special needs. I've taken him to a functional medicine doctor. He goes to a naturopath and a chiropractor. I have him on a dairy-free diet. He's on every vitamin you can imagine. He's gone for neurofeedback. I'm constantly looking at new ways to help him. When I sit down with the school psychologist, she tells me, "You're doing everything you can," and I think, "It's not enough. What else can I do?" It's the same thing with hearing those squeals of not enough. I have to realize it is enough. There are a lot of successes. I have to give myself some credit for the successes that I have had with my perseverance.

Dr. Glenn: How confident do you feel that you're never going to binge again?

Alexandria: I feel pretty confident. Like you said, when someone dies, you want to be like them, but I could draw on the positives instead of the negatives.

Dr. Glenn: You could purposely go over your mom's best traits and think about what you want to incorporate going forward, and you could think about her worst traits that you're going to leave behind. Let those traits die with that generation.

Alexandria: I can do that, because then I'm not going to pass those traits on either. And that's my responsibility.

Dr. Glenn: Now you understand.

Alexandria: I can do this. I've done it before. If you can do it for one day, you can do it for 30. If you can do it for 100 days, you can do it for a year. If I can do it right now for 40 minutes, then I can do it for 40 days.

Dr. Glenn: How confident do you feel?

Alexandria: I'm 100 percent confident. This little 30-year pity party I've been having is over.

Dr. Glenn: What if you screw up like you always did before?

Alexandria: If something happens, I just figure out what Pig squeal I was listening to and move on. If you get a flat tire, you don't slash the other three. You keep going. That's what my mother would say. "Get up. Wipe the blood off. It's just a scraped knee. Move on."

Dr. Glenn: I was provoking you a little bit there. I was hoping you were going to say, "Screw you, Glenn. That's not even a possibility."

Alexandria: I'm not going to screw up. Forget it.

Dr. Glenn: That's the attitude you want to have with your Pig. I was playing with your Pig there, but you gave me the right answer. If you did happen to make a mistake, that's what you would do.

Alexandria: But I'm not going to make a mistake.

Dr. Glenn: The hell with that noise.

Alexandria: I'm not going to let the noise in. I've got better things to think about. I could be so much more productive and creative if I was not sitting here thinking about what I'm eating or not eating and how bad I feel about myself because of something I ate two hours ago. It's just a waste of time. I found this calculator online where you put in two dates and it tells you how much time has passed in between them. I put in the date when I really started having the most struggle with my weight until now, and it was almost 5,000 days. What a waste of time. It's time to end it.

Dr. Glenn: What if you do what you always did before and just go off the diet?

Alexandria: I'm not going to go off it. When we're done with this call, I'm going to build on my 40 minutes and I'm going to make it longer and longer. I'm just not going to listen to my Pig. When it says I can't do it, I'm going to say, "Screw you, Pig." We're done.

Dr. Glenn: Nail that Pig in the cage. Enough with it. Your mother wouldn't put up with it. You don't have to put up with it.

Alexandria: I really don't have to put up with what's in my own head.

CHAPTER 5: WHEN THE PIG WANTS TO BINGE AFTER A "TOUGH DAY"

Introduction

Does your Pig(tm) ever say you've had a "really tough day" and it therefore deserves a big hairy binge? Do you want to discover how to easily resist it?

Interview Audio

https://www.neverbingeagain.com/TheBlog/food-rules/when-the-pig-wants-to-binge-after-a-tough-day/

What to watch for in this Interview

- Setting up food rules to handle night time bingeing
- How to cope with emotional eating and stress eating
- How to deal with eating out and the social pressure of eating with friends
- What to say to your Pig when it urges you to eat so you won't feel stressed or uncomfortable
- How to incorporate drinking into your food plan

Interview Begins Here

Dr. Glenn: What are you trying to accomplish with your diet, and how can I help?

Nancy: I'm trying to bring down inflammation in my body by changing my diet, as well as lose some weight. Also, I have found that I'm less interested in eating animal products, if not for any other reason than sometimes I'm just a bit grossed out by it. I want to look at how I can make a really nourishing, satisfying way of eating that does not include animal products.

I'm not eating any dairy at the moment. I had two little teeny bits of dairy in probably the last 10 days. Over the weekend, the Pig was out a couple of times. The other thing I'm working on at the moment is trying to not eat after my evening meal. For the last couple nights, I've been more successful than I ever have been. I would have dinner, brush my teeth, have some water, do whatever I was into for the evening, and then have a little bit of coconut milk with some pea protein powder when my stomach started growling and I wanted to go for the crackers. That actually worked fine.

That is where I'm at right now. A year from now, I would imagine I would have little or no animal protein at all, limited flour and sugar, and limited refined grains.

There's one thing that is an obstacle with eating more vegetables. I really love beans and rice. I love cruciferous vegetables like broccoli and cabbage. However, I am a massage therapist and I don't digest those foods well. I get gas and that's an issue when I'm working in a small, closed-in space.

Dr. Glenn: Yes, it is.

Nancy: If I'm not going to eat that again, what am I going to eat? I'm a little bit stumped. I don't have easy access to a full kitchen at the moment. I have a microwave, fridge and sink, so that is a little bit limiting in the short term as well.

Dr. Glenn: The flatulence that comes from eating beans is because the gut doesn't have the right bacteria balance to digest it initially. As you eat the beans, it develops that balance and becomes less flatulent. It's a catch-22 because you have the gas until you get there, but how are you going to get there if you don't have the gas? It's a little rough. I don't eat beans as part of my food plan. I just get the calories from fruit. I know it's entirely possible to eat something else instead, but that's up to you. I don't think it's the rice causing the flatulence. It's probably the beans.

Nancy: It most definitely is from my experience. Sometimes, it's caused by cabbage or broccoli. There may be a way around that because most of my massage shifts are in the day. If I include some of these things in my evening meal only, maybe my digestion could adapt without that impacting my work.

Dr. Glenn: What if we charge your patients more on a day that you have beans and you tell them it's a special part of the treatment?

Nancy: Sure, why not? [laughs]

Dr. Glenn: What you want help with right now is to never eat dairy again. "I will never eat dairy again," and then, "I'll never eat after my evening meal again."

Nancy: Maybe this is my Pig talking, but what if you eat at 7:00 or 5:00 and you're not going to bed for four hours and your stomach is churning and growling? My conditional would be that I will allow one cup at the most of a smoothie that's not sugar-laden. I don't want sugar at night. I never used to eat after my evening meal, up until about seven years ago when I moved back to the U.S. after living in Australia for many years.

I'm not sure why I think I can't get back to that place again, except getting to sleep and staying asleep has been an issue for the last five years because of hot flashes, perimenopause and my body changing with age.

Dr. Glenn: Does it harm you to have a no-sugar smoothie later at night? Is it keeping the weight on?

Nancy: I don't think so. I can't imagine a little unsweetened coconut milk with some protein powder that has no sugar or sweetener in it is a problem for the weight.

Dr. Glenn: "I'll never eat anything except a no-sugar smoothie after my evening meal again."

Nancy: Yes. Perfect.

Dr. Glenn: If you have only these two rules in place, is there any other way that your Pig can make trouble for you?

Nancy: When I'm emotionally upset and tired. I fall down when I'm really hungry after leaving my job. I head home on the bus and I get off and go directly to the pizza parlor that I walk by on my way to my apartment. I don't like to rely on cereal bars. I have some dairy-free chia seed bars from places like Trader Joe's, and I will eat those to quell that hunger. The other thing that helps is to have half an apple or a banana on me. I can have that and then get home and cook.

Dr. Glenn: If your Pig couldn't get you to break these two rules, where else could you get in trouble with food? You couldn't have pizza if you were never going to eat dairy again.

Nancy: I actually had a dairy-free pizza with diet cheese the other day. It was excellent.

Dr. Glenn: Does that break your rules in any way?

Nancy: No.

Dr. Glenn: You're happy being able to do that?

Nancy: Yes. I'm not eating a lot of wheat, but as a treat I've got gluten-free bagels that I can eat with some slices of tomato and diet cheese. That would be acceptable instead of going to the pizza parlor on the street.

Dr. Glenn: Do you want to add any more rules to your plan?

Nancy: Eventually, I do. I'm not quite sure what shape that will take. I and/or my Pig are a little bit afraid to put more in place for the next several weeks, but those rules would be around wheat, possibly gluten, refined flour and sugar. I don't feel confident to add those rules. I would really love to have some time to know I can start making these changes. I'm not eating a lot of meat now, so I'm not sure what rule I would put in there. In the past week, I've noticed I'll order something like a stir fry with some chicken in it and then I say, "Why did I do that? I don't even want it." It was just kind of gross to me. I don't know how to put that into a rule.

Dr. Glenn: What is it that you'd want to be eliminating or limiting?

Nancy: Animal products. I'm not doing dairy, so that's mainly burgers, chicken, seafood and bacon.

Dr. Glenn: Are you ready to do that now?

Nancy: I want to wait.

Dr. Glenn: Why would you like to give up dairy entirely and stop eating anything after your evening meal except for a no-sugar smoothie?

Nancy: A Chinese medicine specialist that I consulted with recommended it. Over the years, I've been tested for intolerances or allergies, and dairy always come up. I have been told that inflammation can be a contributing factor to hot flashes. I also tend towards phlegm, and I love to sing. I would really love to see how my body can change with not having the calories from dairy.

I think those are the main ones. It takes off some of the digestive load. I know dairy and animal products are harder to digest than vegetables and other plant-based food types. I think that's important since a lot of our bodily energy is spent on digestion.

In the nighttime, the crunchy cracker binges are trying to fill an emotional need because I'm not feeling satisfied with my life in some ways. And I don't want to use food or some outside substance to deal with that. I would rather address those issues and make changes in my life than use crackers to compensate.

I have gradually been gaining weight since before I left Australia, but when I came back to the U.S. I wasn't at the beach anymore and I wasn't walking all the time. I was in a small mountain town in Colorado where you really had to drive anywhere to get around. I started adding on the weight and eating at night. I don't think it makes anything easier when you have financial stress or other stresses, including perimenopause. Losing weight is also for longevity. Really overweight people aren't in much of a healthy state as they age.

Dr. Glenn: There aren't a lot of heavy 90-year-olds. If you had no dairy whatsoever for a year and never ate after your evening meal except for a no-sugar smoothie, you would have much more digestive ease, you would drop weight, you would breathe clearer and you would have less mucus so you could sing. You'd be dealing with the hot flashes better and have less inflammation in your body. You'd be able to speak up and be more assertive rather than using crackers to squash your feelings. You'd have more energy. Why does your Pig say you need dairy and have to eat after your evening meal?

Nancy: Because I love cheese and crackers, and I would be depriving myself of them. I don't drink coffee very often, but I would miss cream in my decaf. My Pig says that's a comforting, creamy taste. It's soothing in a way. I'm not a huge ice cream fanatic, but once in a while I really like the creaminess of it. My Pig says, "You don't have it very often, so why are you making such a big deal out of this?"

Dr. Glenn: What else?

Nancy: What if a smoothie just isn't enough? What are you going to do then? Go ahead and eat so you're not uncomfortable. What if you're out with friends and they want to have a pizza and it's past your dinner? Don't you want to join along with the crowd and have a taste? You know how yummy and comforting that feels.

Dr. Glenn: Jump back up into your higher self. We gave the Pig a chance. I want to dispute these reasons and come up with better answers. What's a better answer for when the Pig says, "You just love cheese and crackers, and you're going to feel really deprived if you don't have them"?

Nancy: I don't feel great after I've pigged out on a bunch of cheese and crackers. I feel too full and bloated, and I feel guilty for doing it, like I'm a failure. It's not really that comforting, except for maybe the short term.

Dr. Glenn: It's actually discomforting.

Nancy: I don't get a lot of comfort out of it, especially in the longer term.

Dr. Glenn: What about the cream in your decaf?

Nancy: In the past month, after I've had a cup of decaf with some cream, my stomach hurts. It's actually causing me pain in my abdomen.

Dr. Glenn: What about when the Pig says you don't have ice cream that often, so it's not such a big deal this time?

Nancy: Sometimes, I get a stomach ache from ice cream, too. I feel bloated, and if it's later at night the sugar high will keep me up. If I really want something ice creamy, I'm pretty satisfied with a non-dairy version. When I do eat all these things, I'm depriving myself of the increased vitality and mental clarity that comes from abstaining.

Dr. Glenn: What about when the Pig says a smoothie isn't enough if you're working late?

Nancy: Sometimes I mistake thirst for hunger. The other night I had a glass of water. The first thing I should do is go for the water. I was still not quite full, so then I had the smoothie and that was enough. What I want to say to the Pig is I don't need the calories. I don't need the crunch as a way of dealing with whatever is going on in my head. I've got a lot of other resources to go to before giving into the Pig. Let the Pig suffer and be okay with the discomfort.

Dr. Glenn: How confident are you that you're never going to eat dairy and never going to eat anything but a no-sugar smoothie after your evening meal again?

Nancy: I am super confident.

Dr. Glenn: Could you give me a number, one to 100?

Nancy: I'm hesitating. I'm at 99, but I know 99 turns into nothing at all.

Dr. Glenn: Is there a specific reason that you're at 99 and not 100?

Nancy: Yes, there is. Every now and then, if I'm out singing at a jazz jam, I might have a glass of wine that night. That's not a no-calorie item, but it's also not a food item.

Dr. Glenn: Would you like to change the rule a little bit to say, "I will never eat anything but a no-sugar smoothie and/or a glass of wine when I'm out after my evening meal again"?

Nancy: Yes, that makes sense.

Dr. Glenn: How confident are you now?

Nancy: I'm 100 percent confident now.

Dr. Glenn: Is your Pig planning something for you later?

Nancy: I'm not feeling that. This is a Pig-free zone.

CHAPTER 6: BEATING THE CONFUSE AND CONQUER MANEUVER

Introduction

Do you ever feel confused about which diet to follow? One day it's low carb or paleo, the next high carb, macrobiotics, or one of those calorie counting or points systems? Does it ever seem like if you could just stop jumping from diet to diet you might be fine... you just don't know which one to choose because they all seem right AND they all seem wrong? If so, this is the interview for you. Because you're suffering from your Inner Food Demon™'s attempts to Confuse and Conquer you with something I call "The Grass is Greener on the Other Side" syndrome.

Interview Audio

https://www.neverbingeagain.com/TheBlog/food-rules/beating-the-confuse-and-conquer-maneuver/

Things to watch out for in this interview

- How to handle the "I'm not going to lose weight fast enough" Pig squeal
- How to combine Never Binge Again rules with your existing diet to make it even more effective
- How to create a positive, invigorating vision of the future that will help you cage your Pig for good
- How you can inspire your kids to eat healthy and grow

into healthy adults
- How to handle eating in special occasions
- How to be 100% confident that you'll succeed in your diet

Interview Begins Here

Ali: I've had struggles with my weight and overeating my whole life. For the last two or three years, my biggest struggle is I will start an eating plan in the morning, like Whole30, and then by 11:00, I'm starting to think to myself, "This isn't going to work." I'm going to eat so many carbs, and I'm not going to lose weight fast enough. I'm going to be stuck in place, and nothing is going to happen.

So I think maybe I should try this other plan that is less calories and follows the same principles, and I'm on that for an hour before I say, " Well, this isn't really going to work. I guess I should do something else." And I end up eating Twinkies. It's just a constant vicious cycle, and a lot of times I feel like I am never going to lose this weight. I've been 300 pounds and I've been 160 pounds, and it's always been a struggle with controlling what I eat. It's like one bite and I'm off and running.

Dr. Glenn: Do you believe that if you were to follow one plan, even if it were less than perfect, that would be better than jumping from plan to plan?

Ali: I do believe that. If I stuck to something, I would see results. Part of my problem is I think that nothing is fast enough, like I need to lose all this weight by next Monday.

When I did Whole30, I lost 17 pounds in a month. I don't know where I'm getting the idea that it won't work because it did work. It's just this game I play with myself over and over again.

Dr. Glenn: What you're describing is a classic case of the Pig maneuver we call Confuse and Conquer. It's also called the Grass is Greener syndrome: this other diet over there is always better than the one you're on. It keeps you constantly confused about which diet is going to work so that you wind up actually on no diet at all. Chaos can reign, and we can just keep binging.

The way we deal with that is by saying we're not going to allow it, even if one diet is not perfect. If you believe Whole30 nutritionally complete and calorically sufficient enough to work for you, then we're going to commit to that and start to dismiss all the squeals that say, "But it's got this flaw or that flaw," because we know that there are even more flaws in a plan that involves switching from diet to diet.

We're going to give this a good shot for a month and dismiss anything else that says we shouldn't do it as Pig squeal. Is that something you want to do?

Ali: Yes. In my mind, I think I need more than a month, more like 60 or 90 days. That's what I really need to get over a lot of these serious sugar issues. I feel like I paralyze myself and bring myself to this place of feeling so overwhelmed.

I would very much like to just dismiss everything else and say, "This is it. Forget about you." The number seems to be a big thing in my mind. I feel like I need to lose all of this weight now. As it comes off, it comes off. I've got to stop thinking this isn't fast enough or good enough.

Dr. Glenn: If you lose weight too fast, you're going to stimulate your biological drive to hoard calories.

Is Whole30 the plan you would like to execute? We don't need to commit to it yet. I just want to understand.

Ali: There are actually two, and that's part of my problem. When I did Whole30, I felt very healthy, I felt very clearheaded. It was a wonderful plan.

Then there's another plan that follows the same basic tenets, but it's a much more lower calorie plan and it has faster results. You're supposed to follow it for eight to 12 weeks and then take a four-week break before starting up again.

Part of my problem is that Whole30 is wonderful, but maybe it will be faster if I do this other plan instead.

Dr. Glenn: I've almost never had long-term results with people that have had fast weight loss. Maybe one or two people. In my experience, I prefer a plan that goes more slowly and steadily.

Ali: Whole30 is a very good, nutritionally sound plan, but it would be good to include some conditions when I make my food plan because I do have a habit of overdoing things. I really don't need to eat half of a watermelon tonight or I don't need to eat three pounds of cherries. One or two cups is sufficient. Even within Whole30, you need to put some guidelines on what you're going to do.

Dr. Glenn: What are the restrictions you want to add?

Ali: What I would like to add is just to make sure that I include vegetables with at least two out of three meals every day and to not overdose on fruit, which is a problem with me. Once I cut the processed sugars, all of a sudden I'm eating very large quantities of fruit and in some ways that defeats some of the purpose of the plan.

Dr. Glenn: How would you limit the fruit?

Ali: Up to three servings of fruit a day, with a serving being one apple, a cup of watermelon, two cups of cherries, or something like that.

Dr. Glenn: Will your Pig confuse the definition of a serving?

Ali: Like I'm saying, one serving is one apple, not two apples. It's one cup of watermelon or two cups of cherries. It has to be more specific so that I can't get away with sitting down with an enormous bowl of whatever.

Dr. Glenn: Do you need to include any other restrictions on Whole30 to make yourself confident in this plan and keep yourself out of trouble?

Ali: I'm very comfortable with the protein. I'm comfortable with the fat allowances. I'm comfortable with all those things, so that's not an issue. But I do have an extremely big problem with coffee. I drink iced coffees, and I put cream and sugar in them. I can drink two or three of them a day. It's the one thing that seems to always derail me.

When I was on Whole30, I was getting coffee and putting coconut milk and half a banana in the blender just so I would have something. That was okay and it works for me. But the coffee is one thing that I find that I have a really hard time letting go of. I don't know if it's a physical thing or if coffee is a comfort for me when I'm dealing with stress.

Dr. Glenn: What role would you like coffee to play in your life?

Ali: I would like to have it occasionally. I would like to have coffee every now and then, like on the weekends or every other day. I don't really think it's good for my adrenal to drink this much coffee. My sleep cycle gets messed up. I don't want to be reliant on it..

Dr. Glenn: Be more specific. What would be healthy?

Ali: I usually go to Dunkin' Donuts or Starbucks and get an iced cold-brewed coffee. It would be okay if I had one of those every other day, but on Whole30 you can't have any kind of sugar or sweetener. I would have to blend it here at my house, but I feel deprived when I don't have my coffee. It's a mental thing.

Dr. Glenn: If you never have more than one cup of coffee every other calendar day, would that be healthy?

Ali: If I have one coffee every other day, I think that would be fine. I think it would break my dependence on it because it wouldn't be something that I have to have.

Dr. Glenn: If you were to follow this plan for 90 days, could your Pig get you into trouble in any other way?

Ali: The only other thing that I could see the Pig causing trouble with would be potatoes. It sounds so silly when I say it out loud, but like I said, I tend to overdo things. I'm fine with sweet potatoes, but I can eat a pan of regular potatoes. That's not healthy. That's not in the spirit of what I'm trying to do.

Dr. Glenn: How would you like to regulate potatoes?

Ali: Maybe once a week I can have a serving of potatoes, on Saturdays or Sundays.

Dr. Glenn: Is there any other way your Pig could get you into trouble if we followed this plan?

Ali: No, because I'm taking care of the big problems that I encountered on the plan. Everything else was fine.

Dr. Glenn: Put your Pig aside for the moment. I want you to imagine that it's 90 days from now and you've actually done this. As a matter of fact, you've done it perfectly, even though your Pig says you're not going to lose weight fast enough and you better jump to another plan. Can you tell me what's different in your life?

Ali: I feel like crying right now just thinking about that. I would feel incredibly healthier. I find once I get a lot of the junk out of my system, I think more clearly. My moods are more stable and I'm less irritable. I have more energy. My outlook would just be so much more positive. My clothes would be fitting better. I think I would be much, much happier.

Dr. Glenn: How specifically would you be healthier?

Ali: Fortunately, even at my current weight, I don't have any chronic health issues, but I'm sluggish. I don't have a lot of energy. Because I eat so much sugar, I think my blood sugar dips and I get irritable. My sleep cycle is very off. Sometimes, I'll fall asleep at 9:00 and wake up at 11:00. Then I'm up until 3:00 in the morning before I fall back to sleep, and I've got to get up at 7:00 with the kids. It's not a healthy cycle.

My emotional health would improve. My moods would probably level out more. I won't eat a meal all day and all I'm eating is cupcakes and garbage, and then I'm irritable and I snap at the kids. I'm in a bad mood or I feel depressed. I think all that would even out after 90 days.

Dr. Glenn: What would change in your life as a result?

Ali: My relationships with my kids and maybe even with my husband. And my relationship with myself. This is really affecting how I feel about myself. It would change my motivation. I have a lot of ideas about things I want to do, but I'm not doing them because I just don't have the energy or motivation to do them.

When I was on Whole30 previously, I did feel much better and I was more motivated to do stuff.

Dr. Glenn: What kinds of things?

Ali: Physical things, like being more active with the kids. The last time I was on Whole30, I started this Facebook page for parents of children with special needs. We got a really big response from it and it was going so well. Once I went off Whole30, I started feeling lousy and I turned it over to somebody else because I didn't want to do it anymore.

Dr. Glenn: You said your clothes would fit better. Is there a particular dress or a pair of jeans that you're looking forward to wearing?

Ali: I have this skirt I have not been able to fit into in my closet. I probably have a range of sizes that I have grown into and grown out of over the past 10 years, but there's a particular skirt that I would be absolutely thrilled to get into.

Dr. Glenn: What color is it?

Ali: It's black.

Dr. Glenn: When did you get it?

Ali: I got it about nine years ago, and I wore it for some special events that I remember well. I felt really good in it, so I would like to wear it again.

Dr. Glenn: Is there anything else that would be different in 90 days if you follow this plan?

Ali: I would be feeding my kids better. Because I don't eat as well as I could, I don't think I'm feeding them as well as I can. I would like to change that, and that's a big motivator for me, especially with my daughter. She's eight now. I also have a 22-year-old, and she has struggled with her weight her entire life. I feel pretty guilty about that. My eight-year-old doesn't struggle, but I would hate for that to start happening at some point.

Dr. Glenn: You can be a better role model and set her up for success.

Ali: Sometimes we're eating fast food or we're eating out, and it's just not the best thing for her either.

Dr. Glenn: Anything else?

Ali: No, I think I would just feel better and be more confident and happier.

Dr. Glenn: Why don't we give your Pig a chance now? You have this food plan that you feel excited about. We want to commit to it for 90 days no matter what, even if something else seems better. We know all these good things would happen if we stayed on it for 90 days. Why does your Pig say that you can't do this?

Ali: I won't be able to survive 90 days without a cupcake, cannoli or coffee. How can I give all that up? I'm not going to be able to change for the kids. I'm not going to lose weight fast enough. I'm probably going to lose only five pounds anyways, so why put myself through all of this for nothing? I'd lose my stress release. As soon as I get stressed, I run into the kitchen. What am I going to do then? What if we have a special occasion? I'm not going to be able to have a glass of wine or eat the cake. I'll feel deprived. I've failed at everything else already, so why would this be any different?

Dr. Glenn: What I want you to do is jump back up into your higher self and try to give me better answers. Try to tell me what's the truth is. When the Pig says you won't be able to survive 90 days without a cupcake, cannoli or coffee, what's a better answer for that?

Ali: Obviously, I can survive. I've done harder things in life. I'm not going to be like the wicked witch and turn into a pile of ash if I don't get a cupcake.

Dr. Glenn: What were the harder things you've done in life?

Ali: I survived a lot as a kid. I also raised a child by myself, which was tough. I went through some serious losses. Even with a lot of challenges, I managed to make more of a success of myself than a lot of other people in my family.

Dr. Glenn: You went through a lot.

Ali: There were ups and downs, but I've always persevered. I'm a survivor. You do what you have to do. You just keep going.

Dr. Glenn: What about when the Pig says you won't be able to change for the kids?

Ali: Even though my daughter is a perfectly healthy weight, she eats a lot of mac and cheese and grilled cheese. She's not a particularly healthy eater, and I know it's going to be a struggle to turn her around.

Recently, I was thinking that I can't control what she eats. I can't put the food in her mouth, but I can control what I offer her because she is only eight. She doesn't have a credit card. She can't go and buy herself cupcakes or mac and cheese. I can control what I offer her, and if she chooses not to eat it, then that's her choice.

Dr. Glenn: Kids do about 20 percent of what their parents say and 80 percent of what their parents do. Kids need to see their parents make the changes themselves for a year or two before they really come around.

Dr. Glenn: When the Pig says you're not going to lose weight fast enough, what's a better answer to that?

Ali: I'll lose at the pace I lose and eventually I'll get there, but I'm not happy with that answer.

Dr. Glenn: I understand. I work with a guy who started at 500 pounds and he had tried so many times. He lost 100 pounds and he gained it back. Finally, he just said, "I'm going to set up a plan that I could stay on forever, and I'm just going to lose five pounds a month." That's how he did it. Month after month, he just took five pounds off. He felt more and more secure, and he said, "I've just got to do my time. I did my time putting the weight on. I've got to do my time putting the weight off."

I wish I had a faster way that people could take the weight off and keep it off. I know people pay all kinds of money for that, but I just haven't seen people maintain it when they do it that way.

Ali: This has been a lifelong thing with me, since I was maybe five or six years old. I didn't gain this all in the last six months. I went through periods where I was thinner and periods where I was heavier. I got up to 300 pounds. I had gastric bypass surgery in 2000, and I got down to 165 pounds. There were pregnancy and fertility issues, and up and down the weight went.

Then my mother passed away. She was sick in the hospital for two months. I put on 20 pounds in two months, and I haven't lost any of that. The only time the weight came on really fast was when my mom died.

Dr. Glenn: Is there any doctor that's telling you that you have to lose weight really quickly because you're in an emergency situation?

Ali: No. There's no emergency. There is one doctor I have who encourages me to lose weight for my health. I had a physical, and I have no major medical problems. I'm fairly healthy, as far as I know.

Dr. Glenn: I would say lose five to seven pounds a month. Maybe the first month it will come off a little faster because of bloat and water. So, what is a better answer? You spent a lifetime putting this on, and you're going to have to do your time to take it off. The Pig is just going to have to do its time. We're not putting ourselves through all this effort for nothing, we're putting ourselves through it so we can get thin and stay thin.

Ali: Even if I didn't lose one pound, I would be healthier because I would stop eating all these processed foods. I would stop putting my blood sugar through the constant pounding that it takes by fasting all day until 3:00 and then eating three cupcakes and two coffees. Then dinner time rolls around and I have a cheese sandwich, and I start eating at 11:00 at night until 2:00 in the morning. Even if I lose nothing at all, I would be doing myself a service to put nutritional food into my body instead of the processed garbage that I'm eating.

Dr. Glenn: The Pig says you're going to lose your only stress relief mechanism. What's a better answer for that?

Ali: Suck it up and find some other way to deal with your stress. That's a tough one, because I do find myself turning to food very often to deal with stress. When I get stressed, the first thing I'm thinking about is junk food.

Dr. Glenn: If you have six problems and then you binge, now you have seven problems. It's not really a stress relief mechanism. I tell people that they're not really just eating for comfort. The things they're eating are actually getting them high. People don't want to think of themselves getting high with food. They don't want to think of themselves like a drug addict. They want to think that they're comforting themselves, but it's not really true. You're anesthetizing yourself, but you're also seeking the high.

Ali: Instead of drinking wine or taking morphine, I'm eating. Is that what you're saying?

Dr. Glenn: Yes.

Ali: Food is the substance that's getting me high and knocking me out.

Dr. Glenn: When the Pig says you need something different on special occasions, do you agree? Do you want to make a special rule for special occasions?

Ali: No, you can't on Whole30, unless I make my own rules. If I have a birthday party or family event and I want to have one dessert, I will. That doesn't go with Whole30, but then again, it will be easier for me to follow the program if I do something like that.

Dr. Glenn: What specifically would that be?

Ali: If I have a family barbecue where they're serving dessert and wine with dinner, I would have one dessert or one glass of wine.

Dr. Glenn: What constitutes a special occasion?

Ali: A birthday celebration, an engagement party, an anniversary, or other things of that nature.

Dr. Glenn: How often do you want to allow this to happen? Once a month? Once a week?

Ali: Maybe once a month.

Dr. Glenn: When the Pig says you'll feel too deprived, what's a better answer for that?

Ali: I'm depriving myself of feeling good about myself. I'm depriving myself of my health, and I'm depriving my kids of a more balanced mom because I get irritable and snappy. That's a much bigger deprivation than having to skip the chocolate cake.

Dr. Glenn: You're depriving yourself of being a better role model and having a better relationship with yourself, wearing that little black skirt you want to wear, helping the parents with special needs kids, and being more active with your kids.

Ali: In certain situations, like we go out to an amusement park, I have to wonder about, "How am I going to feel in the seat of that ride?" Going clothes shopping, I have to pass up whole racks of clothes because none will fit me. I can't buy the clothes I want to buy. Getting in a car, my son sat next to me and I had a moment of hesitation before I sat down. Is this going to be too tight? Is the seatbelt going to fit? Situations like that don't feel very good.

Dr. Glenn: Your Pig is depriving you of that confidence.

Ali: It deprives me of the confidence just to say, "Let's hop on and go."

Dr. Glenn: When your Pig says you've failed at everything else already and this won't be any different, what's a good answer to that?

Ali: It helps being able set rules for what will and will not happen to take the ambivalence out of it. Maybe just taking the alternatives off the table and saying, "Come what may, we're going to stick with this one approach and ride it out."

Dr. Glenn: The research shows that people that keep trying something new to lose weight eventually figure it out. There's no reason just because a boat has been traveling for miles in one direction that the captain can't turn the wheel if they want to. The past does not dictate the future.

Ali: That sounds like Dr. George Spencer. You create your new future every day.

Dr. Glenn: And Spencer said we can remake ourselves every day, too. How confident are you that you're never going to binge again?

Ali: I feel more confident. I wouldn't say I feel 100 percent, but I feel steadier about it than I felt before.

Dr. Glenn: That's good to hear. What percentage would you give it?

Ali: I don't feel 100 percent, but I do feel much better like more possible.

Dr. Glenn: The reason I keep pushing people to aim towards 100 percent is to see if the Pig has any other thing up its sleeve. It sounds like it doesn't at the moment, but there's a trap that the Pig puts us in that says, "You can't be 100 percent confident until you feel 100 percent confident." I know that sounds like it's true, but it's not.

We can't get rid of the Pig. We can't get rid of our whole history of binging. It's always there, and it's always going to be a pain in the neck. What we can do is 100 percent commit to separate from the Pig. We can say, "I'm 100 percent confident, but my Pig has other ideas."

That installs an algorithm in your head that continually pushes the doubt and insecurity to the Pig, and that gives you more confidence to commit to separating from the Pig. You should not be frightened if you have an impulse or a craving. It's a normal part of the process. We can't get rid of your lizard brain, but you can always translate, "I'm afraid that I might binge," into "The Pig really wants to binge." You can say, "I'm 100 percent confident, and the Pig has other ideas."

The way this game is played, the desire to binge is the Pig's desire, so all of the anxiety and insecurity belongs to the Pig as well. This will help you tremendously if you're willing to make that commitment.

Ali: Sometimes, I hear the voice in my head telling me, "You'll start tomorrow." That's not really me. That's the Pig. I have to be able to recognize when that voice comes up, it's not really me, it's them. That's not the part of me that wants to move forward.

Dr. Glenn: It's your destructive self, and you're choosing to separate from it. Would you be willing to say you're 100 percent confident, even though your Pig has other ideas?

Ali: Yes. I'm 100 percent confident I won't binge again.

CHAPTER 7: WHAT TO DO WHEN FINANCIAL ANXIETY "MAKES" YOU OVEREAT

Introduction

Financial anxiety is rough. Nothing seems to preoccupy the mind like "how am I gonna pay the rent or mortgage". Unfortunately, almost everyone feels this anxiety these days. And you'd better believe your Inner Food Demon(tm) is ruthlessly on the lookout for an opportunity to use this anxiety as an excuse to Binge Eat. Read this intriguing full length interview to hear how I coached Camilla to overcome the urge!

Interview Audio

https://www.neverbingeagain.com/TheBlog/food-rules/interview-what-to-do-when-financial-anxiety-makes-you-overeat/

What to watch for in this Interview

- How to prevent yourself from bingeing on "healthy food"
- How to create "success momentum" to cope with the "Let's eat to stop feeling financially anxious" squeal
- How to not binge when you're offered food (a love gift) at social events

- How to reject "free" food even though your Pig says you have to accept free stuff because of you financial situation
- How to transform the feeling of "drowning under pressure" into a vision of standing up in shallow pool and just walking away

Interview begins here

Dr. Glenn: I understand you got the book, you had a good start and then you've been struggling a little bit.

Camilla: I changed career a year ago and I work from home now. That's where the Pig squeals the most -- when I'm at home working and I feel very anxious about something.

Just to take you back, it's about two months now since I started the food plan. It's low carb, high fat, no flour and no refined sugar. I have a lot of Nevers. After dinner, I never eat at the computer. I never eat pizza, pasta, popcorn, chocolate, dried fruit, bagels, breakfast cereal, Nutella, potato crisps, lollipops, biscuits, bread and cake. They're my trouble foods.

Dr. Glenn: Is there anything else on your plan?

Camilla: I have one always that says I eat at the table or eat sitting down, and a conditional on nuts. There are a few conditional foods that I went back and tried to tweak because they became things that I binged on. I've got one almond a day, but that's been really hard to stick to. Ice cream, once a week. Dark chocolate, once a week. I had frozen berries and fruit as once a day because I love that kind of dessert like. It's a trigger for me. I cannot overeat with fruit.

Dr. Glenn: You'll never eat after dinner. What defines the end of dinner?

Camilla: The plates are back into the kitchen or the kitchen is tidied up and the food away. That's the end of dinner.

Dr. Glenn: How do you define refined sugar?

Camilla: Any sweetener or any artificial sweetener, although I'm still allowed Stevia.

Dr. Glenn: I find people do best when they say something like, "The only sweet tastes I'll ever have again are whole fruit, berries and Stevia." Is that what you mean?

Camilla: Yes.

Dr. Glenn: When you say flour, what defines flour?

Camilla: That's tricky. Flour is grains in general. Rice flour and all those gluten-free flours are included in the flour.

Dr. Glenn: What about almond or soy flour?

Camilla: I have almond and coconut flour.

Dr. Glenn: You'll never eat grains again including flour derivatives from grain, or you'll never have flour again? Can you have rice if you want rice?

Camilla: No, I don't have rice.

Dr. Glenn: Is there any grain that you want to allow yourself, like quinoa?

Camilla: No.

Dr. Glenn: Saying you'll never eat grains again will cover all the flours that you don't want to have, but it would allow for the lower carbohydrate flours like almond or soy flour.

You'll notice I'm adding the words "never again" to most of these rules to make them stronger. The language locks it down a little better. I will never eat at the computer again. I always eat sitting down or I will never eat standing up. I'll phrase it like that. I'll never eat more than 10 nuts in any given calendar day or at a meal. What's the limit there?

Camilla: Per day.

Dr. Glenn: Per calendar day again. I know this can sound obsessive and boring, but it really locks things down so there's no ambiguity. What does it mean to have berries? Do you want to say you'll never eat more than one or two servings?

Camilla: One serving. I have a standard bowl size of frozen berries I'm talking about.

Dr. Glenn: You know what a serving is. There's no ambiguity there.

Camilla: No.

Dr. Glenn: Could your Pig get you to grab a giant bowl and say it's just one bowl? Like a big salad bowl?

Camilla: No. My Pig takes a small bowl and then I fill it and fill it. In my head, I never see the total quantity. That's the trick my Pig plays. I don't see the total mess of what I eat because there are lots of little refills.

Dr. Glenn: When you say you eat very low carbohydrate, do you measure that in some way or is it just that the sum total of all these Nevers prevents you from having too many carbohydrates?

Camilla: I don't measure it currently. I'm a week into following a low-carb recipe plan, which is limiting me to 20 grams of carbohydrates a day. I feel fantastic. It's high-fat, almost ketogenic recipe plan. I don't see myself sticking to this very strict recipe plan for my whole life, but it has shown me I can happily eat very low carb.

Dr. Glenn: We don't need another rule to say how many carbs you're going to have?

Camilla: No.

Dr. Glenn: If you follow these rules 100 percent, is there any other loophole where you'd wind up eating something that you wouldn't be proud of?

Camilla: It's the portion control. I watched one of your videos about binge eating on real food. It's a problem I have, as I can binge on Brussels sprouts. I don't know how to address that because I have got vegetables as unrestricted in my food plan.

Dr. Glenn: In what situation would having too many vegetables be a problem?

Camilla: Only in the sense that I can feel quite uncomfortable. I found eating too many Brussels sprouts does not feel good.

Dr. Glenn: They're not that easy to digest. Are you having them with salt, oil, butter and things like that?

Camilla: Yes.

Dr. Glenn: Would you like to make some type of restriction that will make you feel safer?

Camilla: Yes. How could I put a sensible boundary around healthy, yummy food that I might overeat?

Dr. Glenn: You could say, "I will never eat more than one fistful of sauced vegetables per meal again." While you allow un-limited amounts of un-sauced vegetables, you could still do that. That's one option. What do you think?

Camilla: I like that. With this recipe plan I've been follow-ing, I weigh the amount of vegetables per recipe, and I really like a bit constraint. It makes me happy to know I've got 225 grams of cabbage to eat per meal. I would like a constraint around the vegetable portion.

Dr. Glenn: There's nothing that says you can't weigh and measure it. Some people say that's obsessive. Some people really like it. I used to like that kind of thing.

Camilla: I don't know what amount to use, but I can put a number in.

Dr. Glenn: You can put a number of grams afterwards and you can play with different amounts to see what it actually looks like before you can decide.

Camilla: It will set a healthy upper limit of what would be a reasonable meal-sized vegetable portion.

Dr. Glenn: And then if you want more vegetables, you'll just have them un-sauced?

Camilla: Yes.

Dr. Glenn: "I'll never eat more than X grams of sauced vegetables again." I trust you to do this instead of your Pig, because it will say, "42,000 grams."

Camilla: No.

Dr. Glenn: Are sauced vegetables the only thing you have volume control issues with? I'm assuming you follow the rest of the rules.

Camilla: That's pretty much it. I have Greek yogurt unrestricted. I don't really binge on yogurt.

Dr. Glenn: You can keep your eye on that. Let's put your Pig aside for the moment and assume you eat this way 100 percent for a year. Even though your Pig says that will never happen, let's assume it did. What do you see? What's different in your life?

Camilla: What I really want is the energy and vitality that I'll get from breaking the cycle of sugar up and sugar down. I have a few kilograms to lose, but it's not my primary goal. In a year, I would feel fantastic physically. I have quite a lot of chronic, low-level but annoying health issues related to flour. I get bloated. It upsets my digestion. I have bad Pre-Menstrual tension.

All of that really drags me down. Not only do I beat myself up for binging, I physically feel really terrible. I feel fat because my tummy puffs right out. In a year, all of that would be gone. I'd feel great.

Dr. Glenn: What would you do with all the extra energy and vitality that you'd have?

Camilla: I would be able to focus 100 percent on my new business goal. I started up my own business a year ago and I'm struggling with it. I've got a lot of self-doubt and anxiety about what I'm doing and where I'm going. I really need to be on my game and believe in myself. This underlying issue of addiction is driving my inner critic to say, "You're not good enough." If I can prove to myself in a year that I can stick to this, I will have shown myself that I can do it and I'll have the energy to have a successful, fun online business that earns me $100,000 a year.

Dr. Glenn: When you master your own eating, it gives you the confidence that you can master your own fate. The Pig is probably the worst enemy we've ever faced. If we can overcome that obstacle, then building a six-figure business seems like a piece of cake.

Camilla: Yes. That is absolutely how I feel. I feel like I have this thing dragging me down and I can't get there until I fix this problem.

Dr. Glenn: It's a big Pig on your back. What else would you do with the energy? You'd build this business to $100,000 a year or more, and what else would you do?

Camilla: That happiness and self-belief would help me find a new relationship. I'm single and I would like to find a happy, healthy relationship eventually.

Dr. Glenn: You can kiss the requisite number of frogs before you found your prince?

Camilla: Yes. I had a recent relationship failure and I can see that how I feel about myself is an important part of any relationship. If I'm not happy, then it's hard to be happy in a relationship.

Dr. Glenn: It also makes it possible to attract the right kind people if you're feeling confident about yourself. Anything else you would do with that energy and vitality?

Camilla: It would give me the energy to mend some difficult relationships with my ex-husband and my mother. Not so much mend them, but I could manage them. I'm very passive. I have problems with some people in my life and I feel like I have no energy to cope with it. I just ignore it. I put it away.

Dr. Glenn: Some people take more energy than others, don't they?

Camilla: Some people take a lot more energy than others.

Dr. Glenn: You're saying you'd be able to be more assertive. You'd be able to muster the energy to stand up for your boundaries. I don't want to put words in your mouth, but I think that's what you're saying.

Camilla: I have to stand up for myself.

Dr. Glenn: And deal with the onslaught of difficulty that comes from your mother, your ex-husband or other people in your life who have trained you not to stand up for your boundaries in the first place.

Camilla: Yes.

Dr. Glenn: That's a good one. They're all good, but that's one we don't often hear. What else would you do with all the energy?

Camilla: The other most important thing to me is my daughter. If I'm healthy and not having these sugar swings, I'll be a happier, more loving mother. It's the people who are closest to me, like my daughter, that bear the brunt of the bad days where

I hate myself. It's like a domino effect. Every day I get up in the morning and think today is the day I'm going to get back on track, and then I don't. I'll be a better mother in a year if I stuck to this plan.

Dr. Glenn: Some people talk about being a better role model for their young kids too. Do you have any of those feelings?

Camilla: Definitely. I have a lot of anxiety around what I'm role modeling for her. She might learn all the same food addiction behaviors that I did because of the society she's growing up in. That worries me, so it's important to me to be a good role model.

Dr. Glenn: Let's talk about the low-level health issues related to flour that wouldn't be there anymore. What would it mean to you not to have the bloat, digestive difficulties and pre-menstrual syndrome, and just not to feel so gross anymore

Camilla: It would mean that I'm taking care of my body and I'm investing in my future well-being. Living a long and healthy life is a really big goal of mine. But the short-term goal is just to wake up in the morning and get out of bed feeling well.

Dr. Glenn: Is there anything else that would change in a year if you ate this way 100 percent?

Camilla: I haven't talked about exercise, but I exercise a lot. I'm probably an exercise bulimic, which is a term I've heard you use. In a year, I would like my relationship with exercise to be much more about well-being than an anxiety-driven punishment cycle where I have to exercise after binging. I've been a half-marathon runner for many years, and I am injured at the moment. It's important to keep exercising. There are so many other benefits. Mentally, I get a real buzz and I feel happy from exercise. But I want to get past the anxiety that comes if I haven't exercised today. I want to get rid of the feeling of being a slave to my exercise routine.

Dr. Glenn: Let's bring your Pig back and ask how it's going to get you to break this plan.

Camilla: My Pig squeals are the loudest with this computer work trigger. It's a kind of a panic, actually. I feel like I can't do this and the only thing that will help me is if I get some food. Paradoxically, the food does help me in a very short term. I come back to my desk and I go into a kind of a trance of work, eat, work. I'm mindlessly snacking at my desk. Sometimes, I can't work without having the support of food. The Pig tells me that.

Dr. Glenn: Is that true? Have you had other times when you could manage your work anxiety without Pig slop?

Camilla: I can do it when there are other people around me. I don't know what changes when I'm in a shared working space. I just deal with it. I don't want to be eating Pig slop all the time at my computer. When I'm at home, I obviously feel quite lonely as well. It's another trigger.

Dr. Glenn: It's very brave to be working at home, building a business by yourself as a single woman with a young daughter. I've been an entrepreneur my whole life and I've been supervising entrepreneurs, so I know this backwards and forwards. There are realistic feelings that you have to face as an entrepreneur. It's just part of the game. Anxiety is not going to kill you. I want to give you a question you can ask yourself at those moments to get refocused. It's difficult when you don't have other people around and you realize you're sinking or swimming based on your own efforts.

Ask yourself, "What's the smallest possible step I could take next without any possibility of failure?" Sometimes, that's sitting down and opening a Microsoft Word document and typing three words, even if those three words are just blah, blah, blah. Other times, it's dialing a phone and leaving a message for someone. It can be getting out an educational video you have to watch to learn how to do X, Y or Z. What's the smallest possible step you can take without the possibility of failure?

Fear of failure is really strong. If you know there's something successful you can do, it starts a little momentum and it gets you past the Pig saying this anxiety is intolerable. You just need that moment where you can push the Pig's thoughts away. It's similar to when the Pig talks about how it's going to get you in the future. It says you're going to forget your plan or your mother is going to seduce you into eating this or that. It's not attacking you in the future. It's attacking you in the present moment. All you need to do is say, "I never binge now," and that pushes the thought away. You need little mechanisms for pushing that anxiety away and just getting back to work. Does that make sense to you?

Camilla: Just take one small step, like opening a Word document. That gets you past the feeling of being stuck and helpless. I push that thought away.

Dr. Glenn: Push it away. And anxiety won't kill you. The Pig says you're incapable of tolerating this anxiety, but you're capable of tolerating it. You can be anxious and still do your work, or you can be anxious and not work and just not eat Pig slop. There are lot of options.

If you want to deal with the anxiety, you could go for a run or you could sit and write in your journal. You could go for a walk outside or you could play with your daughter. There are a thousand things you could do to deal with the anxiety besides eating the Pig slop.

Camilla: I'm also thinking a lot about discomfort. There are times when you feel uncomfortable. I'm just trying to learn to accept that.

Dr. Glenn: Life isn't a pain-free experience. The definition of wellness has to do with the ability to accept reality and be present. It doesn't have to do with the ability to be happy about it or be oblivious to the things going on around you. That's why we have the phrase "a happy moron." It's a derogatory phrase. The only way to be happy all the time is to ignore everything. What you want to do is be present and accepting of what is happening and navigate through what life has to offer without having to blunt your feelings and sensations with Pig slop. That's the goal.

Why else does the Pig say you can't do this?

Camilla: The Pig squeals at me when I'm at social gatherings. My worst experiences have been morning tea in somebody's house, or a birthday party where somebody has lovingly prepared cakes and baked goods. I feel this love associated with this food and then I really need to eat it. It's very special and I need to have it. The Pig tells me that somebody has put all this love into it and I need to eat it to show my love for them.

Dr. Glenn: I actually just wrote another book about those kind of social events. What you're feeling is normal. There is a tribal custom of breaking bread that bonds people together and indicates we're interested in being friends, not enemies. We're interested in sharing resources as opposed to competing for them. There is a lot of love that is transferred via the sharing of food, but it's possible to accept the love without accepting the Pig slop. There are many ways you can do that. Let's say my mother comes over with a piece of chocolate pie and says, "I made your favorite. I haven't seen you for six months. Thank you so much for coming over. I made this just for you."

I could say, "Mom, that is so sweet. I can't believe you did that." I could give her a hug and say, "My stomach is a little off right now. Do you have any mint tea?" What you're doing is offering her the opportunity to give you another love gift. I call this the alternative love gift technique. You've given her a hug, so she feels accepted and loved. You've given her a way to express her love that's going to make you feel accepted into the tribe. You're showing her you do want to share resources and break bread together, but just in a different way. But you're not bringing attention to that. If you bring attention to it, it doesn't work.

You're not having an argument about how the chocolate pie is really not good for you or her. You're not making her uncomfortable about what she's eating. You're not making her uncomfortable about the love gift she wants to give you. You're just accepting and loving her before diverting her attention to another way to welcome you into the tribe.

Camilla: That makes sense. I have massive guilt around saying no to food, especially if everybody else says no. Then there's this cake that somebody has made and I feel like somebody has to eat some. That's really ridiculous.

Dr. Glenn: People don't realize culture has inculcated these traditions of eating things that are really killing us all slowly. By the time they hit 60, the average person in our culture is struggling with some type of cardiovascular disease, diabetes, cancer or autoimmune problem that's dietarily influenced, if not dietarily preventable.

If you really love these people, you're not doing them any favor going along with the tradition indefinitely. If you really love these people, the most loving thing to do would be to lead by example and show them that it's really possible to be a loving member of the tribe without ingesting this food. Eventually, they come around. That's how you're going to get them away from the very terrible end that comes of all this.

Camilla: I would love to get past the stage where the people around me think I'm a bit crazy. Why would I try to give up sugar? What's wrong with me? I want them to see my lead and follow when they see the results.

Dr. Glenn: What else does your Pig say?

Camilla: There's one other trigger I can't get my head around. In a work environment, somebody's laid out a lavish morning tea. I feel somebody's brought free food and I can't say no to free food. And it's really nice, expensive free food. I don't get this opportunity very often, so I should have some because I may never get another chance to have something like this again. I don't understand that. What's in my head that says that free food is so great and special?

Dr. Glenn: If you jump back up into your higher self, what would be a better answer to that situation?

Camilla: It's Pig slop. I will regret this. I will feel unwell after I eat this. It will trigger my binging and I'll end up eating more and more. There are a whole bunch of reasons not to do that.

Dr. Glenn: One way to think about it is to say food is only food if it's on your plan. It's not really food if it's off your plan. The other way to look at it is that it's not really free. It's going to cost you all of the things that you just described for me in your future. If you jump off this plan, you're not going to believe in yourself. You'll be off your game, which means it's going to be a lot harder to accomplish your business goal and find a new relationship. It's going to be harder to be a good role model for your daughter and be a happy, loving mother. You're going to feel bloated and have difficult digestion. There's a very significant cost to the food. It's not really free.

I'm zeroing in on your anxiety. You've got entrepreneurial anxiety, which lends itself towards thinking you're going to starve. Men in white coats with mustaches are going to come and take things away. There's not going to be food on the table. You're going to be a really bad mom. Your kid is going to be a bag of bones. [Camilla laughs] See, I'm glad you're laughing. If you remember those images and exaggerate the situation, you realize your Pig is catastrophizing for you and it's silly.

None of that is ever really going to happen. You'd have to push it really far to get thrown out of your house and have those people with white coats and mustaches show up. You'd make some other choices before it got down to that. You would get a part-time job or rely on friends. There's all sorts of things you could do to keep the bottom from really dropping out. It's important you identify the catastrophizing the Pig is throwing at you because it's trying to make you binge. It wants you to be more frightened than you need to be so that you will jump ship and have that "free food."

What else does your Pig say?

Camilla: It's an inner critic who says, "You're a food addict. You failed before, and you'll fail again. It's hopeless. You should just give up."

Dr. Glenn: The Pig wants you to identify as an addict and arrange your whole life around being an addict.

Camilla: LIke you're somehow flawed. You learned these behaviors and you'll never unlearn them.

Dr. Glenn: You know that perception is binge-motivated, right?

Camilla: When you tell me, I see it.

Dr. Glenn: Have you seen scientific evidence that suggests people really can't control themselves around food?

Camilla: No.

Dr. Glenn: Do people who accomplish really great things in the world typically do it on the first try, or do they fail repeatedly before they figure it out?

Camilla: I know that they fail and learn. Each time I fail with my food plan, I'm not going backwards. I am actually taking a step forward. It doesn't feel like that at the time, but I do believe that.

Dr. Glenn: Is there any reason to believe that the ability to get up and fail and get up and fail again is a weakness as opposed to a strength?

Camilla: No. It's not a weakness. It's normal human behavior.

Dr. Glenn: Is this inner critic valid?

Camilla: No.

Dr. Glenn: It just wants to weaken you so you'll binge more.

Camilla: I would love to put it permanently to sleep.

Dr. Glenn: Get an attitude. Say it's going permanently to sleep and it better listen to you or you're going to do worse to it.

Camilla: I love that. Thank you.

Dr. Glenn: How confident are you that you're never going to binge again?

Camilla: I feel really strong right now. It's been really helpful looking at what the future could be like and why I'm doing this. The process can be rough, like going cold turkey or learning a new behavior. I feel like I'm swimming against the tide of cultural and social pressures.

Dr. Glenn: We're deprogramming you. The Pig says it's such an overwhelming tide that you're going to drown. You understand you're not powerless and that you can always use the present moment to be healthy. No matter what the Pig says about the future, it's actually only attacking you in the present. You always want to use the present moment. If you never binge now, you'll never binge again because it's always now.

When you do that, you can step up and stand aside. These industrial foods, the advertising industry and the addiction treatment industry are pretty powerful, but the bottom line is we live in free countries and nobody can force you to open up a bag, take something out of it, put it in your mouth, and chew and swallow it. There are an infinite number of intervening moments between the moment the craving hits and the moment it goes in your mouth. At any point, you can stop the Pig and say, "Back in the cage."

We have the power. It's a matter of getting the focus, clarity and motivation straight, which is what we did today.

Camilla: That resonates with me. Never binge now.

Dr. Glenn: You want to tell yourself you're 100 percent confident, even if the Pig has other ideas. By doing that, you're committing to separating your personal identify from the Pig. You're creating a very clear line between your constructive and destructive thoughts about food. If you keep pushing all of the negative, destructive thoughts onto the Pig, then you're inserting a lever that will give you a choice. And you can definitely make that choice. You have the power to make the right choice at those moments. We can't get rid of the Pig because it's tied to the lizard brain, but we can separate from it.

CHAPTER 8: CAGING THE SANDWICH MONSTER

Introduction

Does your Inner Pig(tm) keep you hooked on sandwiches of one type or another? Hmmmm? read the transcript below...

Interview Audio

https://www.neverbingeagain.com/TheBlog/food-rules/caging-the-sandwich-monster/

Things to watch for in this interview

- How to handle the "It's tasty and convenient" Pig Squeal
- How to deal with the fear you will binge in the future because you've always failed in the past
- How to assign all doubt about your eating to the Pig so you can fully separate from it and control your cravings
- How to handle extremely emotional situations without bingeing
- What to do when the Pig tries to confuse you by creating too many rules

Interview begins here

Dr. Glenn: I understand you read the book. Can you tell me what impact it had on you?

Victoria: It actually had a very profound impact on me because I've been studying the topic of food cravings for quite a long time but I never had thought about it from that perspective. It made things so much clearer in my head because we all know that there's another part of us that's not very good, but your book helped to put a name to it, Pig, and actually separate it from myself. Before, I was thinking there are two parts inside of me and I need to live in peace with both of them. Your book actually helped me to call it a Pig and separate it from myself. That was a profound shift in my thinking.

Dr. Glenn: It's kind of a paradigm shift. In psychology, we thought we had to accept all of ourselves. We thought that for a long time. I was obese for a lot of years because of that thinking. What have you done with it since then?

Victoria: I'm a blogger myself and I teach other women how to lose weight. This craving idea comes up very frequently, so I've been sharing this point of view with my one-on-one clients. I've also been doing some short videos trying to explain how differently we could think about this inner part of us.

While I was talking about this, I was trying to tame my own Pig because I also have problems. How ridiculous it is -- a weight-loss coach who also has her own struggles. I have a few food problems, and hopefully you can help me.

Dr. Glenn: My experience is that most weight-loss coaches have food issues, including myself. That's why I wrote the book. Where can I help you the most?

Victoria: I've been having issues with my Pig for about the past year. They weren't very severe, but it gave me some troubles. I've been on a whole food plant-based diet for over four years. I thought that I've been a good girl and I'm the perfect weight, so maybe I can just go off my plan a little bit. I always have problems with cow's milk cheese, but I thought every once in a while it wouldn't be so bad. I'm 99 percent whole food plant-based, so one time will not hurt. Obviously, that was my Pig's voice. I tried it once and then more frequently and then even more frequently. I struggled really badly because every day I was going to a coffee shop and having a sandwich with cheese.

That's what drives me nuts. I thought, "Why am I doing this?" It's not right for me as a weight-loss coach. I teach my clients not to eat these products and I go and eat them myself. I didn't understand what was happening. Reading the book helped me to reduce these cheese sandwich incidents, but still sometimes it happens.

Dr. Glenn: What would you like to do with cheese?

Victoria: Just quit it completely, once and for all. I would like to never have cheese again between now and the day I die.

Dr. Glenn: Did your Pig get your tongue? Was that scary to say?

Victoria: All the different kinds of cheese started going through my head, because there are so many. Is it hard cheese, Swiss cheese and sliced cheese? Is it cheese on a bread? Is it brie? Is it a cheese spread? What kind of cheese?

Dr. Glenn: Do you want to allow any of those cheeses?

Victoria: The hardest one to give up is the sliced kind that goes in a sandwich. It's the combination of cheese and bread that's so irresistible. I don't really struggle with the others. I live right now in Portugal, and my husband's family has a tradition at Christmas of always having cheese. Eating that one piece of cheese doesn't bother me. It's the sliced one inside the sandwich that's tempting and would be problematic. That's one I would like to quit for sure, once and for all until the end of my life.

Dr. Glenn: What about all the other cheese?

Victoria: All the other cheese is still bad, of course. I know how harmful it is for my health, but if I have it once a year on Christmas day then it's probably not going to be too difficult. I don't want to restrict myself completely. I still want to have some fun.

Dr. Glenn: If you never had sliced cheese in a sandwich again, is there any way that your Pig could use that?

Victoria: Yes, there are a few ways. It's very difficult to find good plant-based whole foods here in Portugal. Everything comes topped either with bacon or with cheese. It's almost like in the U.S., except that in the U.S. vegetarian options are getting more and more popular. Here, there are not so many options. If I travel and I don't have any food with me, then my Pig would definitely tell me, "Oh, come on, it's just one time. It's an exception. You're traveling. Nobody is going to die."

Dr. Glenn: How often do you travel?

Victoria: Not often. Maybe once a month or every two months.

Dr. Glenn: Do you want to allow cheese when you travel?

Victoria: No, I don't. If I look hard enough, I can find something without cheese. I'm not going to die if I don't eat a sandwich. I can always go to the supermarket and buy a banana or bag of trail mix to eat it.

Dr. Glenn: Is it sliced cheese in a sandwich or sliced cheese all by itself? Would you get in trouble with plain sliced cheese?

Victoria: I never eat plain sliced cheese by itself. It's either on white bread or a croissant. I never buy white bread or cheese to bring home. If I go to visit somebody, it's not a typical thing to serve, so it's not a problem there either. It's mostly when I go to a café or a restaurant.

Dr. Glenn: That's very easy to isolate. How else could you be in trouble with cheese?

Victoria: I don't seem to find other ways to get in trouble with cheese. It's these very isolated events.

Dr. Glenn: Imagine that you don't have sliced cheese in a sandwich for the next year. How will your life change?

Victoria: I don't think it will change anything in my physique because I'm in good shape right now. What would change definitely is my conscience. I would be freer and not feel so guilty for teaching other people not to do this while doing it myself. I would just feel relieved.

Dr. Glenn: You'll feel like you have more integrity and you're walking the walk in addition to talking the talk.

Victoria: Yes, because right now I feel like a fraud.

Dr. Glenn: What would feeling more integrity and less guilt do for your life overall?

Victoria: I will be more effective as a coach for sure. I would be able to help more people without hesitating and feeling guilty inside. It definitely would impact my one-on-one client work and my blogging because I will be more open. I probably would share this struggle I'm having with my audience, because I know cheese is one of those foods that actually create a chemical dependence in the brain. It's such a dopamine-provoking food. This actually would be a nice lesson to share, but right now I'm too ashamed to share it with my audience. When I overcome this problem, I definitely would be more outgoing about saying you can get into trouble if you don't watch what you do.

Dr. Glenn: What else is going to change?

Victoria: I think my overall health would change as well because all these one-time events are not actually one-time events. They accumulate over time. If I continue this behavior for a year or two years, it's going to impact my health. I really wholeheartedly believe in the whole food plant-based approach and I think it's the best for my own long-term health. I know that in the long term the cheese doesn't bring me anything good at all.

Dr. Glenn: What might happen if you keep eating sliced cheese in a sandwich in the long term?

Victoria: It's a well-known fact that all dairy products are high in cholesterol and estrogen. They lead to the development of cancer cells, heart disease and Alzheimer's disease. I would like to avoid that. This is just my Pig provoking me.

Dr. Glenn: If we give your Pig a chance here, what are other reasons that it says you should keep that cheese in the sandwich?

Victoria: Because it's tasty, and it's a handy option. Anytime I'm out and I get hungry, it's a very easy option to get. Here in Portugal, coffee shops are everywhere, so it's always available. There's no need to look for any other harder kind of option. And the Pig says that once in a while is not going to hurt.

Dr. Glenn: Your Pig would be willing to risk heart disease and cancer, make you feel guilty and make you less effective as a coach, keep you closed down as a blogger and put your long-term health at risk because it's tasty and convenient.

Victoria: It sounds kind of ridiculous, but that's what my Pig is trying to do.

Dr. Glenn: Pigs are kind of sociopathic. It's the lizard brain. It doesn't know anything about your higher aspirations and goals. It's just a survival drive gone wrong, so we're exposing it for what it is. Are there other things you can find to fill yourself up that are almost as tasty and convenient?

Victoria: There are so many delicious and healthy foods out there that I truly enjoy eating and cooking, like beans, whole grains, salads, vegetables and fruit. Cheese is not something I would die for or give up my future for. It's definitely just the Pig. It's a temporary weakness.

Dr. Glenn: Are you ever going to have sliced cheese in a sandwich again?

Victoria: No.

Dr. Glenn: Are you sure?

Victoria: If the Pig squeals, I just cage it. That's pretty easy because I know its voice.

Dr. Glenn: How confident are you that you are never going to have sliced cheese in a sandwich again between now and the day that you die?

Victoria: I'm 99.9 percent confident.

Dr. Glenn: Where is that 0.1 percent coming from?

Victoria: It's the sneaky Pig that sometimes will get me, if I allow it. Like the other day, I woke up in the morning and decided to not have my breakfast. Usually, I would eat a nice, hearty oatmeal with lots of fruit and nuts, but that day I decided I don't want that. I'm just going to go get dressed and go to a coffee shop. I'm going to get a coffee with a cheese sandwich, and I'm just not going to eat anything else that day. It's a guilty pleasure, and I'm going to pay for it for the rest of the day by not eating anything and then going for a workout. Actually, that's what I did, and I almost lost all my chances on the workout because it was so hard after not eating anything.

Sometimes this Pig just convinces me that it's okay one time. I'm afraid those moments might happen. But I know the drill. I know I have to believe in myself, and I just have to go for it. If it goes south, it's okay. I'm going to recover and jump back on track.

Dr. Glenn: The Pig is always a lurking presence because we can't get rid of it entirely. It's always lurking there so it always wants to throw up that doubt. The trick is to assign it to the Pig. When you say you're afraid that you might binge, you're afraid that you might listen to the Pig. Maybe the idea that as long as you manage your calories and exercise for the day you can do it will be appealing. Switch the language and say, "The Pig really wants me to have a sliced cheese sandwich." And that's enough to affect the separation so that you can remember you have a choice. When you say, "I'm afraid that I might," you're giving the Pig power. When you say the Pig really wants to, you're taking the power away from it.

Victoria: You just actually connected the dots for me right now. Yesterday, I was listening to a psychology podcast and the guy was speaking about acceptance and commitment therapy. He was saying that one thing that helps people to accept their situation is not to fuse with their thoughts. Instead of saying, "I don't feel like doing something," you say, "I have a thought that I don't feel like it." You say it's the Pig that wants that, not me.

Dr. Glenn: Yes, that's exactly right. The separation gives you the cognitive space to make the decision. As this idea takes hold, the people who make mistakes describe it as them having made a conscious choice to let the Pig out of the cage. They lose the sense of powerlessness and their sense of free will starts to return. When their language starts that shift, I know they're getting it and I know it's going to work.

So, how confident are you that you're never going to have a single sliced cheese sandwich between now and the day that you die?

Victoria: One hundred percent. If I hear the voice in my head, I know it's Pig squeal. I just caged the Pig and that's it.

Dr. Glenn: I made a recording that you can get in the free reader bonuses on neverbingeagain.com. It's called the binge anxiety killer. The recording recognizes that the anxiety is really excitement and a wish. It's the Pig's excitement and the Pig's wish. You feel nervous about binging, and the Pig is excited about the possibility of binging. I made that recording so people could carry it around and remember to listen to it at the moment of impulse when you're struggling. That should make all the difference in the world.

Victoria: I have it on my phone, believe it or not. I can listen to it anytime. I chose not to. That's really bad.

Dr. Glenn: You listened to your Pig when it told you not to listen. But you're not going to do that anymore.

Victoria: No.

Dr. Glenn: Does anybody have any questions or observations for Victoria?

Harriet: I think we all have the same sort of thoughts.

Dr. Glenn: Sure, we all do. That's the idea. Who else has something?

Barbara: I just wanted to say that I've been doing well. The program is working.

Dr. Glenn: I'm really happy to hear that. How long have you been doing it now?

Barbara: Since the New Year. I struggled at first, but then as I modified the food plan and got rid of that last trigger, it's been working for about a month.

Dr. Glenn: That's not uncommon. What happens in the beginning is our Pigs say, "This is never going to click. There are just so many things that I can beat you on. There's always going to be another loophole." But the truth is it's kind of like a big cleaning job, like cleaning out your basement. It seems like it's going to take forever, but if you just get all the major stuff out of there you'll be looking at a clean room before you know it. That's how it works. You've just got to be persistent.

Harriet, what are we going to do with your Pig?

Harriet: I don't know because it keeps coming back and it comes back worse and worse every time. I don't know if it's the hormones, but I never had it so bad before. I had a week of binging really uncontrollably with rice cakes and hummus. I don't know what's going on, but I can't control it.

Dr. Glenn: If you say you can't control it, then that's going to be true.

Harriet: I want to control it. I made a really nice food plan. I'm just waiting for the right moment to start it, and it seems as if every day I say today is the first day. Then when the evening comes, I have this really bad need to go and buy rice cakes and hummus. One sort of hummus is not enough. I go to different supermarkets for different sorts of hummus and rice cakes because it's the last time, but it comes back again in the evening. I've never had this before.

Dr. Glenn: Have you talked to your doctor about it?

Harriet: No.

Dr. Glenn: I want you to talk to your doctor because it really might be something physiological.

Harriet: I decided to stop the treatment because I really feel like it's not for me. Also, I'm swollen all the time because of the medication.

Dr. Glenn: What you're describing sounds physiological to me. We can go over your food plan again. Do you think there's a hole in your food plan that your Pig is saying something in particular about?

Harriet: Maybe I've been too strict in a way. I wanted to cut out all fats and I think I probably need some. Maybe that's what is not working for me. I would like to allow one spoon of tahini per day so I can have a dressing I really like with my cucumbers. It will give me a little bit of the fats that I need.

Dr. Glenn: It's certainly possible to make things too strict. There's evidence that the binge response has to do with caloric restriction.

Harriet: I eat enough calories, that's for sure.

Dr. Glenn: You'd like to allow a spoonful of tahini?

Harriet: Yes. I would like a spoonful of tahini every day so I can make this wonderful tahini orange sauce that I really enjoy with cucumbers. I don't know if it was trying to cut that out that made everything go off track or if it was other factors like emotional issues. I was really looking forward to this session because my food plan is ready. I'm ready, and I would really like to get out of this.

Dr. Glenn: When was the last time that you made a mistake?

Harriet: Today.

Dr. Glenn: What time?

Harriet: At 9 o'clock. I knew there was going to be a session today.

Dr. Glenn: Your Pig said you should have one last hurrah. Is it possible that it really could be your last hurrah?

Harriet: Yes, it was my last one.

Dr. Glenn: Is there any grey area in your food plan where you were confused and mistook the Pig squeals for your own thoughts?

Harriet: It wasn't really about thinking. I was just buying it and eating it without thinking, "Is this the Pig?" I just thought I have to do this.

Dr. Glenn: When you took the first bite, did you know it was Pig slop?

Harriet: Yes.

Dr. Glenn: So, this was not necessarily about anything in your food plan?

Harriet: No. Maybe I just felt weak.

Dr. Glenn: What do you want to do about it?

Harriet: I want to be free of this problem.

Dr. Glenn: And what would that look like?

Harriet: From today and until the day that I die, I will never eat rice cakes and hummus again.

Dr. Glenn: Why couldn't you do that?

Harriet: I think I had been in a situation that I had never been in before and I didn't know how to handle it.

Dr. Glenn: Did something change dramatically in your life?

Harriet: Yes. I knew that I cannot have children after three months of trying with assisted reproductive treatment. It's something you have to deal with. My way of dealing with it was through rice cakes and hummus, however ridiculous that sounds.

Dr. Glenn: I'm very sorry to hear that.

Harriet: I have other dreams, so I will move on to them. I have a daughter who is 16, and she also just moved away from home this month. That's also something.

Dr. Glenn: Where did she move?

Harriet: She moved to another house. We have two houses, and I was probably too scary to be around. [laughs] But it's nice. We are very lucky to have this possibility. I have a very nice relationship with her.

Dr. Glenn: When we go through these deep emotional up-heavals there's certainly nothing wrong with feeling emotional and upset. As a matter of fact, it would be abnormal if you didn't feel like that. When we go through these emotional upheavals, it's normal for our Pigs to say, "Let's deal with this the way that we used to. You really need some comfort food." We can't stand having this level of emotion. God forbid that we have these deep emotions. We take in some stuff that's going to require a lot of energy so the nervous system doesn't have the ability to conduct the emotions.

Harriet: Dr. Graham also says that you cannot digest and be emotional at the same time. That's why we tend to eat those fat-tier foods when we have the emotions because then we don't feel anything.

Dr. Glenn: What's really important here is that you're making a conscious decision. If you want to dull your feelings, you can. If you want to let the Pig out so you don't have these feelings, you can, but if you want to never binge again, you can never binge again. It just involves a decision to go through whatever feelings you need to go through, and there are going to be a lot of feelings. Given what you're going through, that's perfectly normal.

Harriet: I just realized now that I should have some help other than rice cakes and hummus to deal with this problem.

Dr. Glenn: Do you have someone to talk to?

Harriet: I will find someone. Don't worry.

Dr. Glenn: I'm not worried because you strike me as a very strong woman. But I think the strong choice here would be to find someone that you could talk to because this is a major life change you're talking about.

Harriet: I just didn't realize that it affected me so much because I've been swimming in this lake of hummus.

Dr. Glenn: You must really need a shower after you swim in a lake of hummus.

Harriet: I'm going to have a shower. I will rinse all of this out.

Dr. Glenn: It will be gone in 24 hours. You know how to do that. Anybody have any thoughts about the relationship between emotions and food and what the Pig is after when it tells us we have to deal with the emotions? Does everybody understand about making that a conscious choice?

Karen: I really like how you said the Pig is saying to Harriet, "You can't get through this without the food. You really should have the food, and you'll feel better." That was very helpful. I thank Harriet for sharing, and I'm sorry to hear about her difficult time.

Dr. Glenn: I remember a woman who ate really healthy even when she got a diagnosis of breast cancer and had to go through radiation. She actually took it on as a measure of pride to cage her Pig as tightly as she could during this horrible time. And she survived and was fine. From then on, she found she had this incredible resolve. If she could get through that without letting her Pig out of the cage, then she could get through anything.

I think we can look at these trials that come upon most of us in our lives at some point as an opportunity to really cage the Pig and come up with a new level of strength that will carry us forward through the rest of our lives.

Victoria, do you want to say something?

Victoria: I can really relate to that voice and how that says, "It's okay, this is the last time," and then it never is the last time. Next time, there is going to be some other excuse. When I wrote you an email about the problem, you said that my Pig is going to squeal really hard so just don't let it out. It's like you were reading my future. It actually started squealing a lot yesterday and today, and so I made it a game. I said, "No way, Pig, I'm not going to let you out."

I went on a quest of looking at other options and I actually was very successful. I found some new places where I could hang out. Because I'm a blogger, I work in cafes. Today, I found two nice places where I could have something other than a cheese sandwich. There is never going to be a last time for my Pig.

Dr. Glenn: Fabulous. Every time someone calls me to make an appointment, I have to tell them to be very careful with their Pig between the time they make the appointment and the time they come to see me. Everybody wants to let their Pig out until they see me.

Victoria: I noticed.

Dr. Glenn: You can control your Pig entirely without me. Karen, you wanted to talk about something?

Karen: I did finally put pen to paper, and I wrote down my plan. I had clear things I understood about never and always and unrestricted. My conditionals are in pretty good shape, but I really struggled with what is in or out for processed food.

A corn tortilla may not a whole food, but it's really not that far off compared to some other things. And what about a vegan mock meat? What if I'm going to have one junk food meal a week? What do you do with all the extra food you just bought if you buy a pack of vegan cheese? You got 10 slices, and now you ate one. I think the Pig wants me to be confused so I won't make any rules. I'm trying to get clear on what I want so I can write down some rules and not be distracted by the Pig.

Dr. Glenn: Do you want to talk a little bit about the types of processed foods that you tend to get in trouble with?

Karen: All of them. I've already got a conditional for re-fined grains and sugar, and I have a conditional limiting that to celebrations, other people's houses, after races, vegan events and one meal per week. It's not very simple. There are an awful lot of conditions, but it's pretty clear and it really knocks out the cakes, cookies and ice creams. That's a big swath to take out in that rule so I feel pretty good about it.

That leaves all the salty snacks and the vegan junk -- the mock meats and mock cheeses. I think those are okay as an occasional treat, but I don't think I should be making a steady diet of them day in and day out. I could probably eat Tofurkey and Chao every day, but that's not healthy.

Dr. Glenn: You might do better not to make a rule that you don't eat any processed food, but to have a list of the processed foods that get you in trouble and another for the ones that you want to eat conditionally. Figure out what are those conditions and put the ones that you have to knock out altogether on the never list. Once you have that whole list, look at the food plan as a whole and see if there's any way to simplify it.

Karen: That's really helpful. There are the foods that I do go off the deep end with and there are the ones I could probably eat more moderately without needing a rule. If I would start with those lists and think a little bit about it, that would be a really good place to go.

Dr. Glenn: Your Pig was trying to keep it all under one um-brella so it could hide some things. And while we do want to make things as simple as possible, we don't want to make them any sim-pler. Let's get them all out and then simplify afterwards.

Karen: That sounds good.

Dr. Glenn: Is there anybody that would like to talk about any-thing else today? What did you want to say, Victoria?

Victoria: I just wanted to make a joke. Karen is probably living in the U.S., and it's a first world problem that you have too much vegan junk.

Karen: Yes.

Victoria: Here in Europe, the vegan lifestyle is very new and we don't have all these substitutes, so I personally don't have that problem.

Karen: When you had the whole discussion of the cheese slices, I was thinking you could just have a piece of vegan Chao on those sandwiches and put salt, but I figured you didn't have that there.

Victoria: It's probably possible to find it, but it's not very good and imported from God knows where. I probably wouldn't want to eat it anyway.

Harriet: I have another question about the food plan. I like to have it lying around, but I don't like to see the list of all the things I don't want to eat, like ketchup or barbeque sauce. I bend it so I don't see the part where all the things that I don't want to eat are written, not because I want to forget them but because I don't want to see them all the time. Is that okay?

Dr. Glenn: That's okay. Your Pig is telling you that if you tempt it you won't be able to control it. Ultimately, I want you to get to the point where you could be sitting in front of a barrel full of rice cakes and hummus and know that no matter how much your Pig is drooling, you would never take a bite.

I want you to get there eventually, but if not having to remind yourself about it every day is helping you bridge that gap for the first weeks that's perfectly fine, as long as you don't forget the rule.

Harriet: It's just that the rest of the plan looks so nice and pretty with the celery and the cucumber, and I don't want to look at all the ugly things.

Dr. Glenn: You might want to clip some images of celery, bananas, cucumbers and all the things that you love to eat, and put them all around your house.

Harriet: But I don't want to have a bottle of ketchup on the other side. It doesn't make me happy to see it there. It does make me happy to see that I don't have any more actually. Those cravings all went away completely.

Dr. Glenn: It sounds like you know yourself really well. There was no ketchup on the savannah. It's not a natural occurrence to have to look at a bottle of ketchup. There's no nutritional need for you to stare at a bottle of ketchup.

CHAPTER 9: DOES YOUR PIG HAVE A.D.D.?

Introduction

Does your Inner Pig have Attention Deficit Disorder? (A.D.D?) Does it make your Food Plan SO complicated it is impossible to follow? Read the interview below to me cut right through that prairie pooh in a heartbeat with Janine's Pig. It didn't stand a chance!

Interview Audio

https://www.neverbingeagain.com/TheBlog/food-rules/1268/

Things to watch for in this interview

- How to deal with "conscious Pig parties", where you can hear the Pig but you decide to let it out of its cage and have a bingeing party anyway.

- How to simplify and tighten your food rules so the Pig can't confuse you and sneak out of its cage

Interview begins here

Dr. Glenn: I'm here to coach you through your difficulties with conscious Pig parties, which are when you can hear the Pig. You know it's the Pig, but you decide you're just going to go ahead anyway and let it have a party. Are you having conscious Pig parties? What are you struggling with?

Janine: I put the plan into place with some food rules that I did extremely well on during the month of April, and then things fell apart. I looked back at my rules just a few minutes ago and realized I am actually following a lot of them, but there are times where just exactly what you said happens. I know full well that I could resist the urge to eat this giant cookie with M&M's and yet I still do it.

Dr. Glenn: Tell me what the rules are.

Janine: The first one is I'll never again buy candy from Bulk Barn or anywhere else and eat it while driving around. I have done this 100 percent, which is absolutely astonishing. I love to buy all these Jujubes and drive around in my car. I have not done that once since I made this rule.

It's kind of fallen apart with the next one, which says I'll never again suffer through the 3:20 to 5:30 binge time again. I find that's the most problematic time. I was going to allow myself a snack of no more than 200 calories during that time, which I sometimes do and sometimes don't. I'll never eat while walking around a mall. I've done that too.

On my never list, I put all these foods that I call the C-foods. There's candy, cookies, cake, crackers, chips, ice cream, and the cheese-related family. I thought that would be easy to remember. I'm a total candy addict, and I have not had any candy at all since I made this rule. That's not so much the case with the other stuff.

Dr. Glenn: I might say, "I'll never eat more than 200 calories between 3:20 p.m. and 5:30 p.m. again."

Janine: That might make more sense.

Dr. Glenn: Just to make sure there are no loopholes in it.

Janine: The community I live in is very sociable and many times there's happy hour. If I'm at home, I usually could do okay, but there's an awful lot of socializing and wine drinking here. That's a problem. But that is a good rule that I would never eat more than 200 calories. That's a better statement.

Dr. Glenn: Are there other rules that you're following or want to follow in your plan?

Janine: Again, this doesn't always work. It failed yesterday. I always eat three regular scheduled meals per day. I'm also allowed morning and afternoon snacks not to exceed 200 calories. Sometimes that works, sometimes it doesn't.

Now, a lot of people talk about eating at night. You had a whole thing about that. I do not have that problem at all. I never eat after supper.

Dr. Glenn: Any other rules?

Janine: I always limit wine consumption to two glasses. That doesn't always work out either. For unrestricted foods, I put fruits, vegetables and whole foods. I'd like to go the vegan route, but I'm getting a lot of resistance from my husband.

I was going to allow myself one treat item per week on Saturdays from the C-categories of cake, cookie, crackers and whatever. In April and May, I did that but lately I haven't been doing it. It's not that I don't know these rules. I do, so I wrote down potential problem foods. Candy of all kinds hasn't been a problem. Crackers with jam, peanut butter or cheese hasn't really been a problem. Pretzels, snack food and chips could be problems. Baking supplies like raisins, cranberries, marshmallows and chocolate chips can be problems. Ice cream, desserts of all kind except pumpkin pie -- which I hate -- and carbs of almost any kind can be problems.

I go back to the idea of socializing. I think that's where the problem comes in.

Dr. Glenn: Because that's all available for socializing. What do you want to do about these problem foods?

Janine: I know I have the ability to say to myself I'm going to follow my rules and I can do that successfully, and yet I was intrigued by what you were saying about how consciously you know that even though it's not happening. I would like to eliminate some of those behaviors.

Dr. Glenn: Which ones?

Janine: Mostly those tied to socializing, like the snack foods. Again, I don't normally have those myself, but if I'm at a friend's place, they always have stuff like crackers, chips and cheese. I know I could eliminate that completely if I went full-bore whole food, plant-based, but I don't know if I'm ready to do that.

Dr. Glenn: What are you ready to do?

Janine: I really am ready to go with my "always" plan where I have three regular scheduled meals per day and also allow myself a snack not to exceed 200 calories and two glasses of wine.

Yesterday and the day before, I got caught. I didn't have anything planned for lunch. I was out, and I ended up eating something that I shouldn't have. It would've been so easy to have thought ahead, but I didn't. Maybe if I can just focus in on the three scheduled meals, two little snacks and two glasses of wine that should alleviate the whole pressure that comes during socializing.

Dr. Glenn: Do you want to talk about where you knew that you were breaking a rule but you decided to go ahead anyway? Do you want to figure out what was going on?

Janine: Yesterday, I was starving. At lunchtime, I ate a so-called healthy cookie from the health food store. I knew that wasn't the right choice, but I was so hungry I couldn't take it.

Then I stopped by a friend's place and I was still hungry. She had some pizza, so I ate a piece of pizza there. When I got home, I had one leftover cookie with these M&M's in it and I ate it. I know that doesn't seem like a huge amount, but a few months ago, that would've sent me right over the edge for days. I can just leave it behind now. I know I screwed up there, but I can carry on. This book has really helped me with that.

I do have attention deficit disorder (ADD), but that's another issue. What I need to do is focus in on something that's doable.

Dr. Glenn: ADD is a legitimate problem, but the Pig is using it as an excuse to prevent you from focusing.

When people have a lot of complicated rules about all these different types of food, there's usually a category of food that would simplify everything. Maybe it's salty, crunchy snacks. Do you know what I'm saying?

Janine: That would be good if it could be simplified under one umbrella.

Dr. Glenn: But you're the one that has to do that. I can speculate with you. I don't want to take away food that you don't want to give up. I understand the C-foods. I understand the three meals a day. I don't really understand what the rules are for the ice cream, desserts, supplements, pretzels, crunchy foods and chips.

Janine: That needs a defined rule, doesn't it? I'm finding too many ways to create an exception.

Dr. Glenn: I think so. When there are lots of different loopholes it's easy for the Pig to say, "It's easier just to eat this thing. Screw this. This is too complicated."

Janine: I didn't think this was too complicated, but now that you've mentioned it, it really is.

Dr. Glenn: What do you want to do other than the three meals a day with nothing in between?

Janine: I'd be thrilled if I could do that.

Dr. Glenn: That's what you'd like to do? Just three meals a day and the 200 calories of snacks in between?

Janine: That's too much leeway. What do I do with 200 calories? Eat pretzels? That's no good. It needs to be more defined.

Dr. Glenn: Let's just talk about typical problem foods. There's sugar. There's flour. There are salty, crunchy things. There are salty, fatty things. What types of sugar do you want to allow in your diet and when?

Janine: I only want to allow one thing, and I know exactly what it is. I want to be able to have brown sugar in my oatmeal in the morning. Other than that, I don't want sugar at all.

Dr. Glenn: "I will never eat sugar again with the exception of brown sugar in my oatmeal." What about whole fruit and berries?

Janine: I don't think I have to restrict that.

Dr. Glenn: I'm just trying to figure out how we're defining sugar. "The only sweet tastes that I'll ever have again are whole fruit, berries and brown sugar in my oatmeal."

Janine: What about one treat a week?

Dr. Glenn: Do you want to allow one treat a week?

Janine: Yes.

Dr. Glenn: The way that would read is, "Other than whole fruit, berries, brown sugar in my oatmeal and one dessert treat per week, I will never eat sugar again."

Janine: That's perfect. That is totally workable.

Dr. Glenn: What role do you want flour to play in your life?

Janine: I've gone through phases of my life where that was probably a bigger problem. It's not really a huge issue, but it would sure solve a lot of problems if I got rid of it. Maybe I should dump flour as well.

Dr. Glenn: Dump it altogether?

Janine: I could do that. It wouldn't bother me any.

Dr. Glenn: That would get rid of pretzels, corn chips and things like that.

Janine: Would it? I'd like to believe that corn chips are not made from flour. They're just made from corn. I know it's not the same thing.

Dr. Glenn: It's up to you. I want to know what you want to do.

Janine: I guess that's the Pig jumping up right there when you said corn chips. I thought that's corn, not flour, but it is still a bad thing.

Dr. Glenn: It depends on what you want to do.

Janine: If I could just wake up and be someone different, I would love to say I can control flour and sugar because those are the two really big things that I have problems with. The salty-crunchy and salty-fatty things are not really an issue for me. I could have a bag of chips in my house for five years and probably never eat it. Some people couldn't have it for five minutes. What I need is a rule that deals with flour and sugar with the exception of brown sugar in my oatmeal and one treat per week. That would eliminate all my C-foods and still make it worthwhile to do.

Dr. Glenn: So, we have the rule for sugar. Under what conditions do you want to allow flour? One treat a week?

Janine: Yes.

Dr. Glenn: Are you counting the flour in pretzels and chips?

Janine: Yes, I will.

Dr. Glenn: The rule will say, "Other than one treat a week, I will never eat flour again." Is it that simple?

Janine: It really is, but that certainly requires some planning and forethought.

Dr. Glenn: How so?

Janine: If you're stuck for food and you're out somewhere, it's hard to find something with no flour. Mind you, there's always a grocery store. You can buy fruit.

Dr. Glenn: And you can carry things with you and you can eat beforehand. You can look at the menu online beforehand and look at the ingredients in addition to the actual menu items.

Janine: Yes, that's absolutely true. Actually, I suppose whole foods is easier if you're going to a grocery store because you can always find something that will work. I'm always worried I'm going to get hungry later.

Dr. Glenn: With the rule for sugar and the rule for flour in place, do you want the three meals a day with nothing in between?

Janine: I don't even need that.

Dr. Glenn: I think that your Pig was leveraging your ADD to totally confuse you.

Janine: Oh, good!

Dr. Glenn: Let's just go over this again. "Other than brown sugar in my oatmeal, whole fruit and berries, and one treat per week, I'll never eat sugar again." "Other than one treat per week, I will never eat flour again."

That's how you simplify a food plan. Sometimes when the food plans get too complicated. The whole goal of this is to avoid having to make a lot of decisions about trouble foods, because then that exhaustion sets in and people can say, "I just can't do this anymore. This is too much. I'm going to let the Pig out."

Janine: It really was too much trouble with all these rules.

Dr. Glenn: Do you want to live with this for a couple of weeks and then we can follow up and see how you do?

Janine: Definitely. I think this could be a winner. You've helped me distill this down to something very straightforward and clear. I'd love to try it for two weeks and just see how I feel because I know I would feel fantastic.

CHAPTER 10: GOING BACK TO WHAT WORKED BEFORE

Introduction

Does your Inner Pig(tm) have you lost in a quagmire of strange rules, confusing diets, and overwhelming decisions... to the point you've got NO idea what might actually work, even though there WAS something which worked quite well for you in the past?

Hmmmmmmmmmmmmmmmmmmmmmmmmmmmmmmm....   I wonder what's going on with THAT noise!!???? Read the interview transcript below...

Interview Audio

https://www.neverbingeagain.com/TheBlog/food-rules/1291/

What to look out for in this interview:
- How to know 100% of the time if the Pig is craving something outside your food rules or if it's actually you
- How to totally separate your higher-thoughts from those of the Pig by adopting a very tough attitude towards it
- One strategy that can help you sleep more so you have much more energy and are better able to cope with the Pig
- How to cope with the stress of those 'first few diet days'

<u>Interview begins here</u>

Dr. Glenn: I understand you're still struggling. Where are you and where would you like to be?

Bryan: It's been about four months since I started the program. For the first couple of months, I thought it was pretty easy, and then suddenly for the last two months I've really struggled. Let's say I crave a milkshake. I feel I am the one that wants to have the milkshake because it's going to make me feel better. I'm not able to say, "No, that's what the Pig wants. It's Pig slop." I think there are maybe some factors outside of the diet like stress. Under stress, I feel like I'm the one that wants the milkshake, not the Pig.

Dr. Glenn: What happened two months ago? How did things change?

Bryan: I had some work stress and insomnia. I have an hour and a half commute, and I would think I'm going to fall asleep if I don't get a soda or something really sugary, which is totally not in my diet. It would be a survival decision. I started breaking the diet gradually from there. I ate that on the way home to stay awake. Maybe I can eat it on the weekend, too. Somehow, I would convince myself it's okay to do that.

Dr. Glenn: What is the actual plan? Does it say no sugar? Why is the milkshake off the plan?

Bryan: I'm trying to do low carb, and milkshakes are not low carb. There are a lot of carbs in a milkshake, donut or any of the really sugary foods I've been craving.

When I started really blowing this diet a couple of months ago, I decided to change to a McDougall diet, which is high starch and high carb. I also eliminated diet soda because some people say the aspartame causes you to be hungry. I eliminated sweets. Everything seemed to get worse, not better.

Until a couple of weeks ago, I was still on the starch diet, and then I went back on low carb. I did pretty good for one week, but this past week I totally cheated on this diet. I can't separate my thin self from the Pig.

Dr. Glenn: It sounds like you're gravitating towards the low carb diet at present. Could you say more specifically what rules would govern that diet?

Bryan: Basically, I stay below 60 carbs a day. I try to get 20 carbs at the most, and that's really just from salad or green, leafy vegetables. Those are the only things that I really allow. I don't allow sugar. I don't allow dairy. I do eat cheese, but it will usually be with a burger. I don't usually eat cheese by itself. Mostly, I eat meat. Actually, I needed to get my rules out and refresh them. That may be one of my problems.

Dr. Glenn: "I'll never eat more than 60 carbohydrates in any given calendar day again," "I'll never eat sugar again," "I'll never drink milk again," and "I'll never eat cheese by itself again." That's the language I would use for the rules. Is there anything else?

Bryan: There's no pasta. There are no starchy vegetables. Those things are not on this diet.

Dr. Glenn: "I'll never eat starchy vegetables. I'll never eat pasta." What about grains?

Bryan: I don't eat grains. I don't have oatmeal. I don't have bread. It's a "never" rule, not a "sometimes" rule.

Dr. Glenn: The way we play this game is by definition. If you're confused about whether the milkshake is the Pig or you, when you look at the rules by definition it's the Pig. Any voice in your head that says you should have sugar again in any form whatsoever is the Pig. That's how we define that.

This might sound obvious, but it's important. When we drift away from those definitions, that's how the Pig confuses us about whether it's us or them speaking. We want to go back to the acid test that tells if it's the Pig or me.

At that point, you could decide you're going to let the Pig out. That's better than feeling like the Pig confused you and got the better of you. Even though we might feel a little bit of shame or guilt about that, we won't have relinquished our power. We'll have maintained a separation between ourselves and the Pig. We're free human beings. With this clarity of focus, we're making conscious decisions. And when you keep making conscious decisions, you eventually figure out it doesn't make sense to keep letting the Pig out. When you weigh the pros and the cons, the pros really line up on the side of keeping the Pig in.

There are a couple of other things that could be going on. Not everybody does well on a low carb diet. If you are on that diet, you need to make sure you are eating frequently enough throughout the day.

It takes a little while for your body to turn the food that you're eating into the glucose that your brain needs. You need to keep up your blood sugar throughout the day because the brain's ability to make decisions is glucose-depleting. Work stress forces a lot of decisions on you. You constantly have to prioritize things, and each one of those decisions takes a lot of brain glucose. If you keep pushing those decisions on yourself, by the end of the day your brain is going to feel like it's starving. It's going to try to force you to be less discriminating.

If you do wind up in that situation, you know you don't have to eat. The brain is actually lying. It's really saying, "I would be a lot more comfortable if we ate something now. We need glucose bad."

We want to take a look at how you prepare for your days. Are you packing enough food? You have a lot of restrictive rules, but do you have any incorporative rules?

Bryan: I haven't been following those rules. I'm doing low carb because it was really successful in the past and my rules were probably much clearer in the past than now. In preparation for the day, I would bring lunch. I would even have a snack to eat on the way home. I think the preparation is something I didn't want to think about.

Dr. Glenn: I'm going to suggest a couple of incorporative rules and you tell me if you'd like to change anything. "I will always review my food plan for the next day in writing before I go to bed." I'm going to call it a hypothetical food plan. Before you go to bed at night, review what the next day has in store for you. Take inventory of what breaks you're going to have, what food resources are available, what you might want to take with you, and don't go to bed until you're prepared for the next day. What do you think?

Bryan: That's what I was doing before, so it does make a lot of sense. I just wasn't thinking of trying it again.

Dr. Glenn: The Pig likes to make us forget about the things that worked. It's really good at that.

Bryan: It's my brain. It's me, but we are just dissociating to be able to stop eating. Talk a little bit more about making the Pig suffer.

Dr. Glenn: Our culture has taught us the reason we overeat is because we don't love ourselves enough. As a consequence, when we feel starving our paradigm is to love ourselves more and open ourselves up to that impulse. It's the opposite of what we want to do. You do want to love yourself. I'm in favor of people loving themselves We have to forgive ourselves for our past. As a matter of fact, the self-castigation and ongoing guilt is actually binge-motivated. It's what the Pig does to beat us down so we feel too weak to resist the next binge.

If you're in a situation where you're starving and the Pig says the only thing that could possibly fix this is a donut or a milkshake, you need to have a very aggressive attitude towards the Pig. You need to say, "Oh, you're suffering? Watch how long I can make you suffer."

Once you wake up, go out and get something that's on your plan. I don't want you starving. I want you to have even blood glucose so you can make these decisions and get through these stressful times. It's okay to make the Pig suffer. The Pig certainly made you suffer for years.

Bryan: That's a good plan. Those moments when I think I want a milkshake are really the Pig talking. I need a more aggressive attitude towards the Pig than just saying, "That's Pig slop, and I don't eat Pig slop." I'm not sure how I'm going to think about that.

Dr. Glenn: "You're uncomfortable, Pig? Good. I'm glad you're uncomfortable. You've made me miserable for years. I'm going to make you miserable."

Bryan: Okay.

Dr. Glenn: It's a temporary strategy to get you through the moment and make the Pig shut up. Understand it as a signal there's something physiologically you didn't take care of that day. You want to analyze the day and see if you have enough food. You can also restore the balance in your brain by walking outside or meditating for a couple of minutes.

Bryan: I used to do that, too. My hunger would go away by just going on a quick walk. On my breaks at work, if I was really craving some chocolate, I would take a walk and that would actually help sometimes.

Dr. Glenn: It will also help restore your brain's ability to deal with the work if you take those breaks. You might think you've got three hours left in the day and 42 decisions to make so you can't afford to go outside. The truth is, you can't afford not to.

Bryan: I've been working through my breaks.

Dr. Glenn: That doesn't surprise me. What else did you do that you might have stopped doing?

Bryan: I definitely want to sleep earlier. For some reason, I'm always up late thinking about problems. I feel like I don't want to go to sleep yet. I'm choosing the wrong strategies to relax my mind.

Dr. Glenn: Has there been anything that does relax your mind in the evening?

Bryan: I used to listen to meditation CDs. That would relax my mind and then usually I would fall asleep right away.

Dr. Glenn: That would be fabulous to reinstitute. Do you want to make it a rule or just a guideline?

Bryan: That probably should be a rule. I'm writing it down as part of my night routine after reviewing the food plan. Once I have the food plan set, I can listen to the meditation CD and I should be able to go to sleep on time. The daily exhaustion is one of the big triggers making me want to eat sugar. My brain wants glucose, like you said.

Dr. Glenn: It doesn't get a chance to restore the neurochemical balance. What else did you use to do?

Bryan: I haven't gone to the gym in a long time now. I used to go to the gym and walk on the treadmill every day for 45 minutes to an hour, and then sit in the sauna for a few minutes. It's a little amount of time, only an hour, and I've been thinking about why I have time to go to the gym. I get home and I'm so tired. I don't want to go to the gym. You can almost say the Pig is convincing me not to go to the gym.

Dr. Glenn: Howie Jacobson talks about the inner sloth. He's putting a program together for us.

Bryan: It's really similar to that. My thin self wants to go to the gym, but the Pig is convincing me not to. "You're too tired. You're not going to have energy. Just relax and act like a sloth."

Dr. Glenn: What do you think about maybe walking on the treadmill for 10 minutes and then hopping in the sauna for 10 minutes?

Bryan: That's doable. That's a short amount of time.

Dr. Glenn: Let's say, "I will do 10 minutes on the treadmill." Should we say five days a week so that you can have a little break if you need?

Bryan: Sure.

Dr. Glenn: Do you need to include the sauna in that rule or is that just a natural outgrowth of going to the gym for the tread-mill?

Bryan: Let's include the sauna because it made me feel re-freshed.

Dr. Glenn: It helps you sweat a little more and get out some of the toxins. What if you get sick? Do you want to go and do 10 minutes on the treadmill really slowly anyway?

Bryan: I've been running on adrenalin at work, so I can't remember the last time I even got sick. Yes, I should still probably do 10 minutes, even if I'm sick. That doesn't seem like that much time.

Dr. Glenn: In terms of incorporative rules, do you need to be sure you're having at least two meals while you're at work? If you review your plan every night, is that going to happen naturally? We don't want to have more rules than we need.

Bryan: If I review the plan at night, I'll eat. I've actually been skipping lunches and breakfasts. Most days, I just have a cup of coffee for breakfast and that's it.

Dr. Glenn: I want you to stop doing that, if you're open to it. If you get breakfast and lunch you're going to feel a lot better, in my opinion.

Let's talk about what will happen in a month's time. Suppose you followed these rules: the low carb diet, planning things out, going to the gym and meditating at night. I know your inner Pig says you can't, but what if you did? What would life be like a month from now?

Bryan: I've done that before. I remember my energy was higher. I was losing weight much easier. I was happier about my lifestyle, and I told people about it. My boss at the time said she started doing the same thing and she lost weight.

Dr. Glenn: Why is it important to you to lose weight more easily?

Bryan: I know I'm in the obese category. I'm much heavier than I should be. I haven't been below 200 pounds in a long time.

Dr. Glenn: What I'm after is your motivation. Being in the obese category is different than why you want to be under 200 pounds. What's in it for you if you're under 200 pounds?

Bryan: I just would feel better about myself. My self-image would just be better. I feel like a failure when I can't lose weight. If I was thinner, I would feel a lot more confident around people. You sometimes think that other people don't like you or accept you when you're overweight. I think people are more accepting of me and I'm more accepting of myself when I'm thinner.

Dr. Glenn: If you were more accepting of yourself and more confident around people, what would I see from the outside? How would that look different?

Bryan: People would see me as happier. A lot of times at work, I think people see me as grumpy. I would just be a happier person.

Dr. Glenn: Your voice lit up when you were talking about your influence on your boss and how she lost weight. Why was that important to you?

Bryan: We don't get along too good at work, but that was one thing that we connected on. At work, it sometimes seems like I can never be good enough, but when she started losing weight, she was telling everybody she was doing this low carb diet because I told her about it. Otherwise, we don't really connect on a lot of levels and a lot of my work stress comes from that.

Dr. Glenn: It took the edge off of her disapproval.

Bryan: Yes.

Dr. Glenn: You'd have more energy. What would you do with that energy?

Bryan: People have asked me to go play basketball or golf with them, and I just don't feel like I have the energy. I don't feel athletic enough to get out there and do these things.

Dr. Glenn: What else? Anything that would change with friends and family, or financially?

Bryan: I'm single, so I think I would feel more confident approaching women. That's a big thing. It's really hard to feel confident with women if you just don't feel like you're measuring up. The standard in society seems to be for people to be thin and in shape. It's really hard to feel like I can approach women. If I do, it's like I'm their brother or friend and can't really get out of the friend zone.

I'd feel healthier and safer about my future. I had cancer about four years ago. It's gone now, but I do worry about when I get older. You don't want to have the cancer come back or have other health problems.

Dr. Glenn: Because we know a lot of cancer feeds on sugar, you'd be less worried about it. If you were to stay with this plan for a whole year and not just 30 days, is there anything else you would add?

Bryan: Part of me still feels like even if I'm thin, everybody else who's thin can have milkshakes and eat pizza, tacos and chocolate. I might be thinking down the road that I would cheat and just gain the weight back again.

Dr. Glenn: If we're looking at your higher self and not your inner Pig, are you saying that you would want to incorporate some of these foods back into your diet if you could stay thin?

Bryan: Yes. That's probably the way I would put it -- not that I would start cheating on the diet, but that I would incorporate those foods back into my diet in a controlled manner so that I'm not totally going back into the Pig lifestyle.

Dr. Glenn: There are some people that do better to get those foods out of their diet entirely, and I happen to be one of those people. I just don't have chocolate. I've tried incorporating it back and every time I do, it's a disaster. But there are a lot of other people in your situation that do fine once they reach their goal weight and start to slowly make diet adjustments. That's up to you.

Bryan: I've lost weight and then incorporated stuff back into the diet while still being able to maintain or even lose weight. I would probably have to be cautious, but I think in the future I'd like to try that.

Dr. Glenn: What I found is that it needs to be very specific parameters. I did know a guy who weighed 700 pounds. He mostly gained the weight on frankfurters. He got down to 180 pounds, which was his goal weight, because he gave up frankfurters entirely. Then he had one frankfurter and he gained all the weight back. People were joking it must have been a big frankfurter. Only you will know if you're capable of adding these things back in or not, but it's possible. We could try adding something in very specific measure at that time.

I'd like you to ask your Pig all of the reasons you won't be able to do this. What does the Pig say?

Bryan: This hasn't worked in the past, or at least over the last two months. Until all these other problems at work are fixed, I should keep off the sweets because that's the best way to get through the day. These are the words I've actually thought, and they really are Pig squeal. If I can fix the insomnia, then I could do a diet. Until then, this is just survival. Eat donuts and milkshakes and chocolate and soda. Those are the things that go through my mind.

Dr. Glenn: What else does the Pig say? This is its chance.

Bryan: I don't think it has much more of an argument than that.

Dr. Glenn: "You're going to die if you don't do this. You'll never get through work otherwise."

Bryan: You feel like you're just going to die if you don't eat these things because that's the only way you can survive right now.

Dr. Glenn: This is a corruption of the survival drive. That's why it feels like you're going to die if you don't do this. That's why there is that moment, no matter how much we talk, when you feel like saying, "Just shut up and give me the chocolate before I kill someone." It's not true, but it feels like that. Feelings aren't facts.

Let's jump back up into your higher brain. When the Pig said, "It hasn't worked in the past. It hasn't worked especially for these last two months. It can't possibly work now," is that true?

Bryan: No. In the past, the low carb diet really did work for me. It did solve the problems that I'm dealing with right now, like low energy, insomnia and other health issues. Losing weight really solved a lot of the problems that the sweets are trying to solve now. The Pig wants to convince me that eating sweets is going to solve these problems, but in the past what actually worked was a low carb diet. That's really what my higher self is saying.

Dr. Glenn: Not only can this can work, but it might be the only thing that that's proven to work for you. Is there anything else that did work?

Bryan: All the things that we talked about today -- low carb diet, exercising and having a routine about what food I'm going to bring to work -- are actually the behaviors that were most successful in the past.

Dr. Glenn: Is it true when the Pig says, "You must keep eating until we fix these problems at work because it's the only way to get through the day. We're not going to survive without donuts, milkshakes, chocolate and soda"?

Bryan: It's not really true. In the moment, it seems like it's helping because the sugar rush helps me get through the day, but it really doesn't help in the long run. There are a lot of long-term disadvantages.

Dr. Glenn: You have energy for about 18 minutes followed by a few hours of a crash. That's how it works. Your body has to do all sorts of things to restore balance unless you have another soda before the 18 minutes is up or a little after 18 minutes is up. You just keep on chasing the dragon like that.

Bryan: Keep sipping on soda all day. That's how I've been doing it.

Dr. Glenn: It's another situation where you have to tell the Pig to suffer. You have to find a way to enjoy making the Pig suffer without its donuts, milkshakes, chocolate and soda.

Bryan: I don't know how to say to the Pig I want to make it suffer.

Dr. Glenn: All you have to do is say no. It says, "We can't survive without chocolate. Give me some chocolate." You say no. "We can't survive without a milkshake. It's the only way to get through this work situation." You say, "No, too bad. Suffer." Your Pig is trying to make it more complicated than it is because it wants you to believe that you're not sophisticated enough to do this.

How confident do you feel that you can execute this plan and not binge for the next 30 days?

Bryan: I'm going to guess above 80 percent. I'm probably 85 percent.

Dr. Glenn: How come? What is the Pig saying?

Bryan: I think it's just because I haven't really been able to do this for the last couple of months. Maybe I've been beating myself up about not being able to stick to the plan. I feel like every day I want to follow this plan, but I just can't make myself do it. I feel like I just have to white-knuckle it through the day, and I don't really want to do that.

Dr. Glenn: You're white-knuckling it because you let go of these other behaviors. There are two parts to it. One is making the Pig suffer, but the part that's even more important is taking care of yourself. That's where the food prep, meditation and going to the gym comes in. If you start doing these things, you're not going to have to white-knuckle it the same way. You're making sure you're having breakfast and lunch, and you won't have to be in as much discomfort and pain throughout the day.

Bryan: It's just getting back into the right routines.

Dr. Glenn: Do you want to do that? Please don't feel pressure from me.

Bryan: I do, and the reason I'm not 100 percent is because I don't know if I'm going to have the energy. But I'm just going to have to try.

Dr. Glenn: The Pig says you won't have the energy and you haven't been able to do it so far, so you will fail in the future. Let's look at the energy. When you were involved with these routines before, did you have enough energy to get through your day?

Bryan: Usually in the beginning I don't, but I just do it and then it becomes part of the routine after a few days. For example, the craving for sweets usually goes away after just maybe three or four days. It's those three or four days I have to get through. I keep hitting reset. I go through two or three days, and then on that third day right before those cravings are supposed to go away, I break the diet. Then I have to start it all over again.

Dr. Glenn: What do you think about planning to eat a little extra during the first five days?

Bryan: I could try that.

Dr. Glenn: Even if you're not really hungry, just eat a little bit extra so you don't have as many cravings.

Bryan: I haven't tried that before.

Dr. Glenn: Who cares if you lose weight during the first week? What's really important is to get you on this plan.

Bryan: It makes sense to do it that way.

Dr. Glenn: The Pig says you haven't done it in the past or you're going to continue to fail. What percentage of people who've been successful at something were successful on the first try?

Bryan: Probably not too many. They always give the example of Thomas Edison and the light bulb.

Dr. Glenn: Winners keep getting up. The psychology of winning is to fall down seven times and get up eight times. It certainly was like that for me. I had to fall down a whole bunch of times to figure it out. If I were to ask you how confident you are now, what would you say?

Bryan: I'm pretty confident in my ability to do this because I've done it before. My confidence is high.

Dr. Glenn: You're talking about the last part, which I call the leap of faith. The reason it's a leap of faith is because the lizard brain is always there. The Pig is always there, and we all know there'll be some time when the craving comes back, even if it diminishes as you stop feeding it. We can't cut the lizard brain out of our head because we need it to survive. It's just been misdirected, and there's always that underlying angst that says, "It could take over if I decide to let it." What we can do is commit to a separation of our human identities from this thing we have to live with.

The format that takes in language is saying you're 100 percent confident. It's a leap of faith because you're never going to feel right saying you're 100 percent confident. If you say, "I'm 100 percent confident, but my Pig has other ideas," you've committed to a separation. Keep changing your language so that whenever any doubt comes up, you word it as the Pig's desire. "I'm afraid the Pig really wants to binge."

You say, "I'm not my Pig." You've installed an algorithm in your head that will continue to separate your constructive and destructive thoughts. You'll identify more and more with the constructive thoughts. The leap of faith here is to say, "I'm 100 percent confident, but my Pig has other ideas."

Bryan: That makes sense. I can say it that way. My Pig has other ideas, but I'm 100 percent confident I can do this.

Dr. Glenn: Good for you! You'll continue to solidify if you commit to that idea.

CHAPTER 11: DOES TRYING TO FEED YOUR CHILDREN "MAKE" YOU OVEREAT?

Introduction

Does your Inner Pig™ say that you simply CAN'T eat healthy because of conflicts which arise from having to feed your children?

Hmmmmmmmmmmmmmmmmmmmmmmmmmmmmmm....   I wonder if this is true.... Read the interview transcript below...

Interview Audio

https://www.neverbingeagain.com/TheBlog/food-rules/does-trying-to-feed-your-children-make-you-overeat/

Things to watch out for in this interview:

- How to build your food plan so you get momentum and confidence
- How to make your Pig weaker and smaller every time it squeals for slop
- How to handle social situations where you're offered food
- How to handle leftovers and food that the kids make or bring home

Interview begins here

Dr. Glenn: I understand you read that book and it intrigued you in some ways.

Carla: Yes, it did.

Dr. Glenn: After reading the book, what was it that you thought I might be able to help you with?

Carla: I really like the idea of a Pig living inside me. I totally get what you're saying in the book as far as the Pig's voice and my own voice, so I could recognize that voice pretty easily. But I think ignoring it will be very challenging. I'm hoping you can help me learn how to do that.

Dr. Glenn: Help you deal with your Pig's assertion that you can't ignore it and you must obey its commands?

Carla: Yes. I might recognize when the Pig says something, but I just can't make myself ignore it.

Dr. Glenn: Even though you're becoming aware of the Pig's destructive thoughts and intentions, it's difficult for you to choose to do otherwise.

Carla: Exactly.

Dr. Glenn: I'm using a subtle language switch to help you gain a little more control. When you listen to this conversation again, I think you'll understand.

When I work with people who describe what you're describing, we find it's usually best to come up with one very simple rule that gives them a lot of protection against their worst trigger food or behavior. They find that to be motivating and empowering, and then that provides the momentum to work on the rest of the food plan. It can be overwhelming to try to nail everything down all at once and come up with a plan to protect them from every single problem food.

I usually like to start by asking what their worst trigger is, and we come up with a way to control that. Once they do that, they find it really empowering and they can move forward.

Carla: That sounds like something that would help me.

Dr. Glenn: What gets you in trouble the most?

Carla: Anything sweet and baked, like cookies, brownies and cakes.

Dr. Glenn: Sweet and baked would not include flour or pizza. It wouldn't include bagels or bread. It would include things that have both flour and sugar at the same time. When do you tend to have that?

Carla: Usually only when there is something available. I'm working in a bakery as a part-time job right now, so anytime I'm there the temptation is huge. If there's nothing in my house I'm not going to get in my car and drive to the store to buy something like that, but I will often substitute with something that's also not good to satisfy that craving.

Dr. Glenn: Would you, as opposed to your Pig, be happier if you eliminated sweet baked goods for the rest of your life or would you prefer to have a conditional rule that allows you to have them in some situations?

Carla: I probably would be better off never having them again, but that's the scariest thought ever. My Pig immediately says, "You can do it conditionally because you're not overweight. You don't have any health problems." That's the problem. The fact that my Pig says that every single time is probably a sign that it would be a good idea to eliminate sweet baked goods completely.

Dr. Glenn: Let's think about how you feel about eliminating them completely and then we'll think about how your Pig feels about it. If you were to eliminate sweet baked goods for the rest of your natural life, what would that do for you personally? How would your life change?

Carla: I would have this really great feeling of accomplishment and feel really good about myself. I do have small problems that might go away with eliminating that kind of food.

Dr. Glenn: Like what?

Carla: Like recurring canker sores and stiffness in my joints. The reason I think those would go away is because I did eliminate most sugar and white flour from my diet for six months a few years ago and those problems disappeared. I have a feeling that they would disappear again.

Dr. Glenn: How did you feel during those six months when those problems were gone?

Carla: Really proud of myself and really in control of my health and wellbeing. I felt light, and I lost a couple pounds. I had a sense of feeling in control and feeling really good about my decisions and my ability to ignore these cravings.

Dr. Glenn: What do you think it would feel like if you maintained that for five years?

Carla: It would be awesome.

Dr. Glenn: Can you visualize that? What would your body feel like? What would happen to your life?

Carla: You asked me earlier how it would look if I eliminated that from my life. I started with the positives, but there is a negative that pops up as well, which is that it's really hard. It was when I did it before. It's really hard for me to be around other people who don't know this about me or don't really buy into it. In five years, I would feel really strong and proud of myself, but at the same time, I would feel other people see me as being too rigid and too careful around food.

Dr. Glenn: You would need to develop some new social skills to deal with a little bit of social awkwardness.

Carla: Probably.

Dr. Glenn: I want to stick with how you feel about it and all the positive things you would be giving up if you continue to eat baked goods together like that. Is there any other positive outcome that would occur?

Carla: I read a lot of different books about sugar and white flour and I really believe on an intellectual level that sugar is pretty much a poison. It doesn't help our bodies in any way, and white flour has very little, if anything good for you as well. I know that the inside of my body would be singing and happy. Even though I can't see anything happening on the outside, I know that on the inside it's really good. It's what my body would want.

Dr. Glenn: You would be cleaner inside. You wouldn't be dealing with the toxic byproducts of sugar, the glycemic highs and lows, and all the negative consequences of when you put that into your body.

If you were to stop eating baked goods entirely for the rest of your natural life, what would your Pig be giving up?

Carla: The Pig would be giving up the pleasure of the taste. When my Pig wins the battle, it just has this sense of happiness that it got what it wanted.

Dr. Glenn: That 18 minutes of heaven during the sugar high.

Carla: Exactly. Well, it doesn't last that long. It's more like five minutes and then the guilt kicks in.

Dr. Glenn: You see what kind of a creature the Pig is. It would sacrifice all the things you talked about just just for that five minutes of heaven.

Carla: Even five minutes is probably longer than it really is. My Pig is strong. Everyone's probably is.

Dr. Glenn: It's not any stronger than you are. I say that as a bio-logical fact without knowing you very well. I know the way we're wired and I know what's going on with the hyper-concentrated sources of calories and energy that generate that five-minute high. I've worked with enough people and I've read enough lit-erature to understand that no matter how powerless the Pig has made you feel in the past, you're still biologically superior be-cause that's the way we're wired. The Pig comes from the lizard brain, or the mid-brain. Neurologically, we're wired so that our higher selves can take control. If our higher selves couldn't take control, we wouldn't have a society. People would be driven by their instinct for pleasure to run up and kiss other people in the street or go and steal food out of a restaurant.

I know for a fact you can do this. There is a lot of messaging in society that suggests you are powerless to resist. There's a lot of social pressure to indulge, but it can all be overcome. Can your Pig give you any other reason for giving up all the things you talked about besides the fact that it tastes so good?

Carla: No, I can't think of any other reasons. If I give in to the food my Pig gets stronger. The Pig is happy because it won, so it will win again. The Pig feels stronger and I feel weaker every time it wins.

Dr. Glenn: That's also a physiological fact. You program your reward pathways each time you give in, and every time you give in it gets a little stronger. Correspondingly, every time you put the Pig in the cage, it gets a little bit easier and the cage gets stronger.

Carla: I have one more positive to add. I've read a lot about nutrition overall for years now and I know this is the best way to eat for my body. It just feels like the right thing to do. This is I should act to be the best me I can be, and yet I've been unable to reach that goal.

Dr. Glenn: You want to bring your behavior in line with your knowledge and values.

It's a mild form of torture that exists in all of us. We accumulate knowledge and goals that we know are within reach, but when there's a disparity between them and how we're behaving, we can't be comfortable. We can't ever really feel whole.

Carla: I want to follow this way of eating, and I can't seem to take that last step.

Dr. Glenn: But your Pig would give up all of that. Your Pig would give up the confidence and the integrity of living the values you've accumulated. It would be willing to have you suffer with canker sores and who knows what later in life when your body breaks down from all that junk. It would give up all that for five minutes of heaven. Do you want to let it do that anymore?

Carla: No. I don't.

Dr. Glenn: Would you like to create a rule that says that you will never eat baked goods again?

Carla: I'd like to try. I should say yes, but my Pig is screaming at me right now.

Dr. Glenn: That's exactly what's supposed to happen. It's almost like there are two of you inside your head. It's good you're becoming very aware of this battle, and here's how we're going to win it. We can win if we decided to draw a line in the sand and say, "Carla will never eat baked goods again." It's that simple. All those doubts and insecurities -- it's going to be too socially awkward or it's too tempting -- we're going to assign to the Pig. We're going to decide that all comes from the Pig.

If you wait to feel 100 percent like you can do it, it will never happen. Do you remember in the book I wrote about how you would encourage your daughter or son to climb a mountain or pedal up a hill? We're going to put all possibility of failure out of our mind. We're going to pedal up that hill as hard as we can and we're going to make it. But if we don't, we're just going to get up and do it again. We're going to take a look at what went wrong and see if we have to adjust the rule. That way, you can absolutely climb that hill. It's just an exercise in free will and responsibility. That's all it is.

With that in mind, I'd like to ask you some questions that will force your Pig to the surface. You're going to feel uncomfortable, but it's your Pig that's experiencing the discomfort. I want you to remember that. Are you ever going to eat baked goods again between now and the day you die?

Carla: No.

Dr. Glenn: How confident are you about that?

Carla: About 25 percent.

Dr. Glenn: And where is that other 75 percent coming from?

Carla: The Pig.

Dr. Glenn: What is the Pig saying?

Carla: It's saying, "Tell him no because that's what he wants to hear, but when it's your birthday in a couple months, you can go ahead and have something good because you'll have succeeded for two months by then and you deserve a celebration," and then it goes on and on. A thousand things just popped into my head. I'm at somebody's house, and they don't know that I'm sugar- and flour-free. They made something just for me and I would hurt their feelings horribly if I didn't have it.

Dr. Glenn: What else is your Pig saying?

Carla: Here's the big one. I hate wasting things. If my daughters made some cookies but decided they've had too many and they're going to toss them, I should eat them because that's a waste. They put in all that effort, so I better eat them.

Here's one: I see something that I've never tasted before. All bakeries make things a little different, and I have to taste some at each bakery because I'm head of the bakery. And if I walk by a bakery that's rated number one, I'm drawn to go in. I have to try this particular thing because I've never had it from this bakery. It's okay because I'll never be here again. I can just have it, just this once. That happens especially often when I'm traveling.

This is the reason my Pig is saying I won't succeed.

Dr. Glenn: You told me that you'll never have baked goods again for the rest of your natural life. Your Pig has a whole list of reasons of why that's impossible.

Carla: There's another reason. When people give me sweet baked goods, I feel obligated to eat them or at least try a little to taste before I can give the rest to someone else. I can't just give away un-tasted because I'm curious. I like trying new things. I can't not try it because then I'm missing out on life.

Dr. Glenn: Let's f jump back into Carla's head and address these one at a time. The first one was you should tell me anything to get through this call. You can get through this call and then you can do what you want. That's what the Pig said. What would help you to ignore that?

Carla: Trying to focus more on the positives that I listed before. I have an advantage here because I did succeed for around six months and I felt great. If I can focus on remembering how great that was, it would maybe help.

Dr. Glenn: You felt better than great because you got rid of the canker sores. By the way, I have the same experience. When I cheated, I would get these awful sores in my mouth and they would last seven to 10 days. It made it hard for me to speak. I do public speaking and sometimes I would sound like an idiot on these recordings.

Carla: Luckily, I'm not a public speaker. But it hurts to talk and eat. Of course, it didn't stop me from eating.

Dr. Glenn: It didn't stop you from eating. We're going to change that language.

Carla: Physically and mentally, it feels great. I know that more than just intellectually. I know that from memory. I can tap into that.

Dr. Glenn: Of course, your Pig will immediately say, "One day you're going to forget to remind yourself," and then that's going to be an opportunity. Just ignore that.

Let's talk about the social situations. Your Pig says it's the worst insult to not eat the muffin or cake that someone baked for you. The person will never forgive you and you'll ruin the relationship forever. How could you look at that differently?

Carla: What if I made something for someone and they didn't eat it? I think I would feel a little disappointed. Maybe even a lot disappointed. But I don't think it would last for very long. I certainly wouldn't hold a grudge. It's not something to lose any sleep over. I don't think it's a very big deal. The biggest problem is not necessarily someone who knows me as much as someone who doesn't. When you're invited to someone's house when you're traveling, they make something amazing and you say, "No, thank you, I don't eat that." That's a hard one.

Dr. Glenn: Do you want me to help you with that?

Carla: Yes, please.

Dr. Glenn: In those situations, the person really wants to be acknowledged for how sweet they were and how much thought and energy they put into making this for you. They want to feel loved for having presented you with this gift. When someone presents me with something like that, I say, "That is so sweet of you. How did you make it? This is exactly what I like. You remembered my taste." I just focus on that. I don't eat it, and if they ask why, I say, "I really should have told you about this before, but I'm on a new medical program and I'm really not supposed to eat this now. But I want to take it home or take a picture of it. It's just so sweet." They usually laugh and say, "Sorry, I didn't know."

That way, they got what they wanted. They wanted to be loved, and this was their expression of love. There's no reason to reject their expression of love just because you can't swallow it.

Carla: I see how that works. Maybe you can even smell it and say how delicious it smells.

Dr. Glenn: I don't know that I've gone that far. That sounds great. You're capable of smelling it without eating it.

Carla: I can.

Dr. Glenn: The other thing to remember is that if the person really loves you, then they would want you to be healthy. They would want to support your higher self. Now, you have to be careful to avoid getting into too big of a discussion because they may feel ambivalent about what they're eating as well. They haven't read this book and they don't have this philosophy. If you try too hard to explain to them -- "I have a Pig inside me, and you have a Pig inside you, too" -- they'll just feel insulted. Don't get into any of that. Just make them feel loved.

Carla: I have been eating whole food plant-based for a while, and even that gets touchy sometimes when you start talking about it. I feel like they think I'm judging them, and I'm certainly not trying to do that. They may think I'm looking at them eating all this stuff and thinking how wrong they are.

Dr. Glenn: Having worked with over a thousand people, I can tell you for a fact that there's nobody out there who doesn't have some significant struggle with food. It's a very hot issue. Everybody has got their own thoughts about what they should and shouldn't eat. Everybody wants everybody else to eat exactly the way they're eating because it would be easier for them.

Carla: It's like religion.

Dr. Glenn: What about the idea that the only way you could possibly celebrate your birthday is by having some baked goods?

Carla: I think I could find delicious things that aren't flour and sugar that would satisfy me. You put a frozen banana in a blender with some cocoa powder, and it's amazing. It tastes like chocolate banana ice cream. It's delicious.

Dr. Glenn: That sounds really good.

Carla: I experimented a lot with raw desserts, like grinding up nuts and adding cocoa powder and dates for sweetener. It makes these chocolatey things that are really good. That's not a flour-sugar combo, so that would be okay. I can be completely satisfied with that kind of stuff if it's available.

Dr. Glenn: Why wouldn't it be available on your birthday?

Carla: Because maybe I think it's my birthday so I shouldn't have to make my own dessert. Maybe no one is willing to do it for me.

Dr. Glenn: Your Pig thinks that you shouldn't give yourself a birthday gift.

Carla: My Pig thinks that everyone else should take care of me on my birthday.

Dr. Glenn: That's probably true if we were running the world. It can never be the best of all scenarios.

Carla: I know how to get around it anyway. I would just make it a day ahead of time because then I'm not actually working on my birthday, I'm just reaping the rewards with my work from the day before.

Dr. Glenn: Is there any other reason your Pig says you're going to have baked goods again?.

Carla: If my son brings home a leftover birthday cake from a party, before it gets tossed, I would have to eat it.

Dr. Glenn: The Pig says you have to use your own body as the garbage can as opposed to the garbage can.

Carla: I've heard that before. You're putting garbage in your body or you're putting it in the trash can. Why would you put it in your body?

Dr. Glenn: As you go forward, each day you can ask your Pig what reasons it can think of for you to ever have baked goods again. You don't always have to dispute it. I'm working very hard with you to reframe these things so that you understand how transparent the Pig is about this. In the beginning, it won't be as natural for you to reframe everything the Pig comes up with, but just articulating its reasons will give you protection. At least you can recognize when it's talking and then you can tell yourself, "I will write about this later when I can figure out the right answer," or "I'll just ignore it."

Even if the Pig comes up with a reason you can't dispute, you know what its intentions are. We went through everything you're going to be giving up just to have that five minutes of heaven. You know that you're going to be giving up on your life. Your Pig doesn't care because it's a little bit sociopathic. Even if it comes up with a really good reason for doing what it wants to do, you still don't let it because it's a sociopath.

Are you ever going to have even one bite of baked goods between now and the day that you die?

Carla: No.

Dr. Glenn: How confident are you?

Carla: Maybe 35 percent.

Dr. Glenn: I understand exactly what's going on. The Pig is very loud in your head. At this point, you want to arbitrarily set your confidence at 100 percent. You are 100 percent confident and the Pig can be 100 percent confident that it's going to get you to binge later on. But this way you'll know that whatever reason it comes up with is coming from the Pig. That's the whole point.

Carla: The reason my number is not higher is because my Pig is screaming at me right now. It's saying, " Why did you even say you have to cut it out 100 percent? What was that? You were supposed to say you were going to do it conditionally. What were you doing? That's ridiculous. Of course you can do this condition- ally. You have good self-control." It was just screaming at me loud and clear while you were asking me how confident I was.

Dr. Glenn: Do you want to eliminate baked goods from your life, or do you want to come up with a conditional rule for baked goods?

Carla: I would like to be able to come up with a condi- tional rule, but I am not so sure that I can. As soon as I do that, the floodgates open up and I have 5,000 conditions. It probably would backfire.

Dr. Glenn: That's my sense of things from what you're describ- ing. Are you willing to go forward with this and see how it goes for a couple of weeks?

Carla: Yes, I am.

Dr. Glenn: Now, this is a part you can keep secret from your Pig. You can change your food plan whenever you want to -- not impulsively, but with serious consideration and forethought.

Carla: I forgot until you reminded me. That actually makes me feel a lot better, but that might be my Pig.

Dr. Glenn: We're going to leave as if it will never change and as- sign any doubt to the Pig for the moment. You follow up with me in a couple of weeks, and we'll see what happens. How confident are you that you're never going to have even one bite of baked goods between now and the day that you die?

Carla: I think I'm up to 50 percent now.

Dr. Glenn: Your Pig won't let you say 100 percent.

Carla: It's a lifetime. That's a long time.

Dr. Glenn: The Pig thinks you're going to die without it.

Carla: The other thing is that the Pig lasts for such a short time. Like you were saying, there are a few minutes of pleasure and then it ruins all those good feelings. Those good feelings are there all the time. They're there anytime I think about my eating if I'm sticking to the no sugar and flour rule. Those feelings of accomplishment and strength are there every waking moment as long as I'm thinking about them. That's a really long lasting good feeling, and yet the Pig wants to just throw it all away for a minute.

Another thing is that when I take my first bite, I'm flooded with deliciousness and really good feeling in my mouth. The taste buds are going crazy. But then the second bite is less amazing, and then the third is even less, and it goes on. I'm just eating because it's there. I know I like it, but by the tenth bite I'm not even enjoying it. It's not even five minutes of pleasure. It's that first bite that tis the most pleasurable, but it's the shoddiest pleasure.

Dr. Glenn: That's a really good point.

Carla: If you had a stopwatch and you timed how long that pleasure lasted compared to that feeling of accomplishment, it's so small. It's just a little pleasure in your mouth. I'm not sure if I have a mental pleasure, and that's not even mentioning the good feelings from not having canker sores or headaches. It's such a tiny portion of my life when the food is actually giving me pleasure.

Dr. Glenn: It's the difference between long-term genuine contentment and short-term mania.

Carla: When I think about it, I feel I could totally go my whole life without eating it again.

Dr. Glenn: Would you be willing to say that you are 100 percent confident that you'll never have baked goods again between now and the day that you die?

Carla: I'll say I am 100 percent confident that I can go for the rest of my life without eating a baked good. My Pig doesn't agree.

Dr. Glenn: That's exactly right. Now you got it.

Carla: I can do that.

Dr. Glenn: Too bad for the Pig.

Carla: I think what clicked for me just now is realizing that I am not my Pig. We're really intertwined, but we are two separate entities and I am stronger than it.

Dr. Glenn: That's exactly it.

Carla: I remember reading that, but I didn't really feel it. Right now, I feel like it's true.

Made in the USA
Middletown, DE
19 June 2019